The Book of Iya And The End of Existential Imperialism

By: Tanehesi the Restorer

Table of Content

Oh, how I remember that day

When those AfRaKaNs walked the plank

Oh, how I remember Goree

When those AfRaKaNs walked the plank

So many drowned in the Great Ocean

Are those AfRaKaNs who walked the plank

So many kept their devotion

Are those AfRaKaNs who walked the plank

Now many live in the States

as those AfRaKaNs who walked the plank

Must never make the mistake and forget

Those AfRaKans who walked the plank

Useful Yoruba & Medu Neter Terms

- Cousin-Egbon
- female cousin = Egbon Obinrin
- Aunt /Aunts - ANTI/Awon Anti
- Uncle -Aburo
- Family – Ebi
- Ambassador or Prophet - Asoju
- Parents - Obi
- Sage - Babalowu
- Warrior - Jagunjagun
- Hathor - Hut Heru - House of Heru
- Mother/Your Mother - Iyah - iya re Mut-Netjer (mwt-nTr)
- Father - Igbo Nna re - It-Netjer (it-nTr)
- Sister – arabinrin
- Brother - Arakunrin
- Wife - Iyawo
- Husband Oko

- Female - Obinrin
- Male - Okunrin
- Daughter - Omobinrin
- Son - Omo
- Children: awon omo wowo
- Divine Feminine - Orisha
- Divine Masculine - Olorin
- Divine Principles - awon ilana atorunwa
- Goodbye - Odaboo
- Queen - Ayaba
- king - Oba
- person - Eniyan
- Feminine - Ibawi Abo
- he - Oun
- Universe - agbaye
- galaxy - ajoorawo
- black hole - dudu iho
- she -oun
- her - re

- him - oun
- ancestors - awon Nna nla
- history - itan - Pr Ankh - pr ankh pr
- friends – oro

CHAPTER 1
INTRODUCTION

Years ago, when the book by Molefi Asante entitled The AfRacentric Idea was first released, some considered it to be one of the most radical pieces of literature of its time. Even then, I never truly realized that the American mindset had produced an environment in America that was/is completely anti-African in essence. As a result of experiencing a heart attack, death, and a coma, I was forced to accept certain realities, and as an AfRaKan writer/scholar/activist who attempts to capture the particular circumstances of AfRaKan people with the intent of advocating a method for liberation, I began to understand in my recovery that this process could still lead to the other proponents or advocates of such liberation struggles as being labeled pejoratively or having her/his works referred to as "radical" and "extreme." Especially in those cases where the writer represents the way of thinking that does not reinforce the major appeals to Asiatic existential hegemonic thought.

In other words, when these writers attempt to assert a new way of viewing ideas and their historical development, they do so at the risk of being ostracized by mainstream scholarship and culture as well. Furthermore, the distinction that arises between them signifies a somewhat morbid social connotation. For example, an AfRaKan person is considered radical if she/he desires liberation immediately; a moderate/ liberal if twenty years is not too long to wait on "changes in the system"; a conservative if she/ he couldn't care less about AfRaKan liberation; and finally, a "sellout" if all of the above applies and the person in question does everything in her/his power to work against the liberation struggles of AfRaKan people.

In order to avoid rushing towards an uncritical acceptance of a generalized notion of AfRaKan centeredness, an AfRacentric idea and all references reflecting the idea of an AfRaKan centering should be evaluated. The difference here is that instead of appealing to mainstream scholarship for the legitimating factor in determining the relevance of our ideas, we must move to arm ourselves with an AfRaKan centeredness and proceed to our own world realities.

It is my sincere belief that this process includes a direct confrontation with what has become known as Western Philosophy, AfRacentricity, and AfRaKan Studies with the goal of moving towards AfRaKan/human liberation through the restoration of AfRaKan and other human centerings.

Therefore, radical or 'liberal,' e.g., cannot be the sole factor in determining the relevance of AfRaKan scholarship as well as appeals to the West. It is not to suggest that the references do not have significance because sometimes they are helpful. Our concern is to verify that an AfRacentric movement is more than an intellectual and social pursuit. Thus, outlining an AfRaKan· reappraisal of a worldly orientation helps us raise humanity's consciousness to a higher level and restore and defend the integrity of AfRaKan people.

Paradoxically, our attempt is to move within our AfRaKan base appraising its characteristics and developing a renewed AfRaKan identity which remains something that was uniquely AfRaKan produced as opposed to evaluating AfRaKanity with the goal of arguing for "Westernization".

Historically, it is the renewal of the AfRacentric movement, i.e., the realization of prophecy in the true sense of a religious and prophetic tradition, as is the case with AfRaKaNs and AfRaKans in America, that demonstrates for AfRaKans, in general, the necessity of having a pan-AfRaKan worldview on solutions. It also shows how AfRaKan people divided and dispersed throughout the world have invoked an idea through the symbolic power of existential consciousness that manifests within them the tools required to liberate themselves from the constraints of Eurasian oppression. So that the perspective is clearly understood at the start of this dialogue, it must be clearly understood what we use the reference Eurasian and not white as there is no such thing as a "White" person. In fact, the people that are referred to as such are also known as Caucasians because they are indeed also Asiatics as the Caucasus Mountains, their place of origins is indeed in Asia.

"The Caucasus Mountains[a] is a mountain range at the intersection of Europe and Asia. Stretching between the Black Sea and the Caspian Sea, it is surrounded by the Caucasus region and is home to Mount Elbrus, the highest peak in Europe at 5,642 metres (18,510 ft.) above sea level." Wikipedia

This clearly shows that you have those that refer to themselves as Asiatic "Black" men and those that refer to themselves as Asiatic White men as well. Partially then, it has become the duty of AfRacentrism to create an orientation that contains the innate meaning of AfRaKanity within it. However, it is essential to remember the importance of flexibility in conceptualization.

Methodologically, transcendence is preferred to temporal definitions because it allows us to escape the immediate powers of defining by the moment and the creation of concepts that become static.

The next phenomenon of immediate importance is to consider why most have criticized the possibility of an AfRaKan centeredness because of an initial or surface confrontation between an "AfRacentrism" and a

"Asiatic-centrism" and have dismissed AfRacentricity as a response to Caucasianity. On occasion, we are responsible for demonstrating that there is more behind the shadow that surrounds AfRacentrism. For instance, AfRacentrism is not strictly confined to a materialist conception of reality, as is the case with the major Caucasian intellectual concerns.

Therefore, by critiquing Asiatic-centrism collectively, we can demonstrate how the materialist nature of the Asiatic metaphysical approach to reality differs from an AfRaKan centered approach to reality. Of course, this means that we are responsible for defining our own reality as it resurfaces in our AfRaKan renewal. Afterward, we can then argue that it remains impossible to limit a conception of AfRacentrism to a reaction to Asiatic-centrism. Yet, we must successfully show that AfRacenteredness comes out of an AfRaKan historical context which encounters Europe and the various forms of colonialism much later in history.

The final and most pressing concern leads us in the direction of methodology, and here, the work of Cheikh Anta Diop becomes useful. We can use him to offer an alternative view of AfRaKan history, where we then initiate our analysis. If understood by AfRaKan and AfRaKan American thinkers (pan AfRaKan intellectuals), clarity of method could allow them to regain control of the definitional parameters of an AfRaKan Studies discipline. This is because in methodology, all content pertaining to thought is appropriated, distributed, and reappropriated, creating the structures responsible for ascribing a host of values, norms, and specific characteristics about reality. However, one should not confuse the finger pointing with what the finger points towards. Even though it is generally not perceived as such, culture, religion, and spirituality are all methical, while sometimes being pseudo and unscientific. They produce and reinforce certain systematic beliefs and not knowledge having a very negative effect on consciousness.

In the case of AfRaKa, colonialism, in the form of crude materialism, has dismantled AfRaKan cultural institutions, and now we are accepting Eurasian culture or AfRaKanized Eurasian culture as its so-called progressive replacement. We are discovering through painstaking trials that Eurasian methods are inapplicable as "tools" on other approaches to existential understanding because they tend to destroy uniqueness in existential forms when they leave the confines of their appropriate Eurasian boundaries.

In summary, an AfRacentric methodology must make strenuous effort at dealing with the impact of colonialism/existential imperialism on the AfRaKan mind and existence at large. Here we uncover the responsibility of AfRaKan thinkers for resurrecting AfRaKan studies as they clash with utilizing the current trends in Eurasian thought as the formative basis of AfRaKan thought or exploring new worlds through the re-investigation of traditional, i.e., prior to the arrival of disruptive and colonial forms of AfRaKan thought. They begin by entertaining the question of what is definitively "AfRaKan" and "Eurasian" or "Occidental", especially in terms of the transmigration of ideas from the AfRaKan continent. The questioning strongly confronts the missionary attempts to convert or bring AfRaKans to Eurasian religions. An AfRaKan method can rightly contest and make the world acknowledge Africa's contributions to world religions. Instinctively, a genuine AfRacentric methodology must grasp the foundations of the ancient world, engage in a critique of the colonized version of AfRaKan, relativize contemporary AfRaKan and AfRaKan American Philosophy and remain imbedded in Pan-AfRaKan movements towards liberation that asserts an AfRaKan version of Africa while rejecting the colonized version. Its procession should not initiate from today's Africa but must come to it instead. Reconstructing an ancient AfRaKan reference point is theoretically essential because the most powerful manifestation of an AfRacentrism is its ability to utilize in investigation primary and ancient AfRaKan resources to restore an AfRaKan world view. A centering if it is to exist must emanate from within AfRaKan language, culture thought patterns and religion.

Therefore, an AfRaKan centered method, though conscious of geographical location, promotes an understanding of cultural emanations as they appear in world culture. Thus, for practical purposes, it becomes helpful for AfRaKans in Brazil, for example, to understand how it came that they find themselves in Brazil practicing AfRaKan culture.

It also could explain the various political conflicts now prevalent in AfRaKa. The current political environment in AfRaKa finds various states disintegrating on ethnic lines in the name of democracy. Some states represent realities that were imposed on indigenous peoples and have historically represented the interests of foreigners and colonial powers. To demonstrate that AfRaKa never had political boundaries before colonialism and to deal with the presence of political boundaries is essential.

The method becomes very important in determining the success or failure of the AfRaKan interpreter to remain AfRaKan centered. Of course, there shall be much room for more ongoing research and writing in this area at the end of this project. However, the major emphasis of this project is to bridge the gap between philosophy, AfRacentrism, and AfRaKan studies. Hopefully, with the effort of the magnificent others who have contributed significantly to human endeavors like AfRaKan scholarship, this project will be able to demonstrate respect for their accomplishments. It is evident that AfRaKan people have been some of the most humanitarian people on the planet and have suffered the most disrespect.

Nevertheless, Frantz Fanon attempted to warn us of the imminent dangers that could result if we allowed our dependency on Eurasia to continue. It is certain that Fanon understood the importance of political and economic independence and our existential consciousness and intellectual autonomy. Beyond the Caucasian/AfRaKan confrontation, although there lies a deeper battle between the AfRaKan and her/his own self-understanding. A unique AfRaKan centered method will allow for a minor conflict where Eurasia is decentered, and solutions promoting other alternatives are chosen. The time has arrived for AfRaKan studies to be liberated and for Philosophy to arise from the ashes of death through a total rebirth. In my opinion, an AfRaKan centered method can serve that purpose and reinforce the constructive spiritual orientation to the reality that is already AfRaKan.

CHAPTER II:

THE MAJOR CONCERNS WITH CAUCASIAN METHODS AND THE CREATION OF A FALSE CANON

It is evident from the present conditions of the AfRaKan world that any critique of Asiatic-centrism, which disregards a critique of colonialism, cannot serve as a critique of Asiatic-centrism. Therefore, it is imperative to devote time and effort to reassessing Asiatic-centrism to include the impact of colonialism on AfRaKa. A review of Asiatic-centrism must be accomplished as a parameter in the development of AfRaKan Studies and must also include political, social, economic, and spiritual dimensions. Philosophy should return to serve its purpose as the balancer between these dimensions. In the recent activities that have been labeled "philosophical", the problem has been that, in recent human history, harmony has been forced to give way to individuality and conflict. The dissection of life forms into categories has somewhat destroyed the perception of life in terms of its greater symbolic movement towards wholisms. What needs to happen in AfRaKan Studies is a philosophical revolution that, because of its magnitude, becomes capable of totally restructuring the discipline as it is practiced. The search for a method that captures the transcendent nature of Ancient thought is vital.

A clear and transcendent method in AfRaKan Studies can show the impact of Western methods on AfRaKan Studies and how it has dictated most of the modern AfRaKan philosophical concerns. For example, it can expose how one-dimensional materialist thought has taken the place of AfRaKan concepts of MAAT or harmony. The preoccupation with materialism is not a characteristic of traditional AfRaKan thought. Through domination, Eurasia was able to inject itself as superior and perpetuated false notions of a universal model of human civilization. Eurasia also commissioned a host of intellectuals to reconstruct human history to justify its exploitation of the rest of the world. The most significant development to come out of this "intellectualism", are the various theories of "progression" which necessarily lead to the classification of Ancient societies by their modes of production; said to be either tributary or communal, and making up the central and peripheral societies in the Marxian sense, and finally, the classification of societies as culturally and intellectually inferior to Eurasia's cultural centers.

One of the co-products of our analysis is an evaluation of the constant propagation of the connection between the Eurasian world and Greece. Eurasian renaissance scholars might have attributed more to the Ionians, Socrates/Plato, and Aristotle than they rightfully deserve. When viewed through a different prism, the mythical connection was made possible by the efforts of the Eurasian-centered scholars to disconnect Greece from its Mediterranean heritage and, after that, claim that Greek civilization was Caucasian only. The fabrication of the Greek world was accomplished in complete opposition to its apparent associations with Kemet (Egypt) and Persia (the Orient).. In Marx's historical materialism, for example, tributary societies like Egypt and Persia do not have a distinct mode of production. Therefore, the explanation for Euro-Greco connection is that the Greeks are considered to take the necessary and progressive measures forward in organizing a pre-capitalist mode which Europe turns into complete capitalism.

Nevertheless, the fabrication of the Greek model, and Europe's inheritance of it, remains a modern misconception that becomes fully understandable when we look at what gets labeled the pre-capitalist world.

Reviewing the origins of Greek civilization enables us to construct a "paradigm freed from culturalist distortion." In other words, by declaring the "Age of Antiquity" to be a plural reality, we immediately notice an alternative model of human civilizations. Generally, the casually accepted model of eniyan history promoted the perception that civilizations existed in relative isolation surrounded by widespread barbarity in the ancient world. During this period, societies could be classified as consisting of two types; the central societies are characterized by their tributary mode of production, and the peripheral societies are characterized by a communal mode of production. This would make it almost impossible to establish common traits among these cultures and also impossible to break down the medieval construct of an isolated Greek civilization.(1)

Existing during the same period, however, are numerous mythologies that correspond to the various societies in question. The most common idea that permeates these mythologies is considered by Samir Amin to be a product of Kemet (Egypt):

> Before any other people, the Nykemet (Egyptians) introduce the concept of eternal life and immanent moral justice, opening the way for humanist universalism. Everywhere else, including pre-Hellenistic Greece, the status of what one will later call the "soul "and the fate of the human being after death remains uncertain and vague.(2)

Samir Amin considers the Egyptian breakthrough to be one of universal morality and a reflection of Egyptian social thought. He also suggests that there is nothing during this period of civilization that can be said to represent scientific pretensions. But the concept(s) which gets categorized as science cannot be disparaged from various activities in Kemet(Egypt). Very carefully, we have to distinguish between references like "the Nykemy (Egyptians) had science and philosophy" because we don't need to rush into the uncritical acceptance of what is meant by "science" or "philosophy". As a matter of fact, that is exactly what we need to contest, i.e., ascribing pre-contextual notions on ancient analysis. To avoid this error, we should let the people of Kemet(Egypt) speak for themselves as they have done. Nevertheless, for Amin, the Greeks advanced the foundations of scientific methodology by abstracting a philosophy of nature and social thought that is adopted much later during the medieval period in Europe. Robert Brumbaugh has written on the Greek origins of science that

> Instead of science, there was nothing at all, unless we count technology and calculation, which were necessary precursors of science. It is true that, in the Near East, the Babylonians had done remarkable work in astronomical record-keeping and calculation: but astrology was the direction they took when they looked beyond their tables for any further "explanations." Pure mathematics, as distinct from applied, was not yet discovered. Though some Babylonian tablets do preserve interesting patterns of

solution for some types of equations, they do not represent pure mathematics. The Nykemet (Egyptians), despite some modern admirers of the occult who relate the history of the world to the measurements of the pyramid of Khufu, had no science of a pure sort at all. Ancient Kemet (Egypt) seems a case of a civilization with high standards of technology, art, and culture, but with none of the scientific components that become so important to the West.(3)

Therefore, Greek thought designates a qualitative leap forward for civilization in the eyes of those who buy the progressive model of civilization. The consequence of Greek thought is a separation between metaphysics and the philosophy of nature that grounds an empiricist/materialist art or later science. Hellenistic philosophy becomes preoccupied with the search for the general laws that govern nature. Thus, most scholars like Amin and Brumbaugh conclude that the Greeks established the methods of science.(4)

Nevertheless, reservations are to be held because the prejudice in favor of the Greeks and the West are definitely obvious. Especially since even in terms of Western "science," pyramid building, iron smelting, embalming of its citizens after death, and Egyptian architecture still remain very remarkable accomplishments in the history of recorded civilization. But the West has also borrowed heavily from others. The Greeks inherited many contributions from its neighbors, and their significance to Greek culture has been passed off in modern historiography. In fact, to his credit, Amin argues that Greek civilization is inherently a Mediterranean phenomenon as opposed to a Caucasian one. Hellenism, he says, should be seen as a conglomerate of Egyptian metaphysics, Chaldean mythology and astrology, and Greek innovations in abstract thought. Kemet(Egypt), Greece, and Persia make up the central tributary societies. What is known as Europe had not become an active participant in human civilization during this period of history. After the 16th century, the debate about the originality of the Greek culture became a serious methodological problem for the Caucasian intellectual world.

As a matter of fact, the Enlightenment surfaced when Caucasians attempted to appropriate ideas borrowed from AfRaKan, Asian, and Arabic sources and at the same time was trying to develop a theory of race that would allow them to justify the progression of humanity towards Caucasian superiority and deny that AfRaKaN people made significant contributions to history. What becomes the dividing line in Caucasian "intellectualism" is when some scholars helped adamantly perpetuate the myth of AfRaKan barbarism, and other Eurasian scholars tended not to agree. Therefore, the battle of race; the origin of the Egyptians, their civilization, and its evident influence on Greece; all become particular Caucasian dilemmas that AfRaKans, Asians, and Arabs were forced to inherit as an attack on their humanity. The reason being that it was difficult for Europe, which becomes extremely race-oriented, to conceive that their supposed parent had been influenced by AfRaKans and Asians. They found it difficult to argue race and accept this fact, so they ingeniously dismissed it as a factor.

Even the cultural and religious wars throughout medieval Europe resonate around the theme of superiority and dominance of who in Europe was closer to the Greeks or the Romans.

Martin Bernal's Black Athena becomes a fascinating text regarding intellectual clashes in 16th, 17th, and 18th century Europe. First, he offers a philological analysis of the impact of Nykemey (Egyptian) and Semitic cultures and languages on Greece. Bernal then moves to argue that the idea of "progression" served as a direct attack on the Ancient model or version of human history.

> The Ancient Model was the conventional view among Greeks in the Classical and Hellenistic ages. According to it, Greek culture had arisen as the result of colonization, around 1500 B.C., by Nykemet (Egyptians) and Phoenicians who had civilized the native inhabitants. (5)

Hellomania, as it surfaced in Europe, purposely elevated Greece as the center of complete and unabridged liberties. The fascination of Caucasian scholars with Plato and Aristotle grew out of a need to capture what they identified as the impetus behind Hellenism: the pursuit of human excellence and the highest good. Thus Greek thought is presented as a monolithic tradition that leads from Thales to Aristotle and his students and represents the quest to acquire real knowledge.

In the ancient world, Hellenism and the attempt by Alexander to unite the worlds of Egypt, Persia, and Greece under one empire produced a profound effect on the region. In this respect, Christianity and later on its estranged offspring, Islam, are said to have evolved as religious reinterpretations of Hellenistic metaphysics and a result of the opposition to the social order imposed by Alexander, which justified Greek thought. The societies under analysis can be characterized as they had to deal with the following:

> There is the latent, permanent conflict between the people and authority, which bears all the characteristics of the class struggle characteristic of tributary societies. The people (peasants and small craftspeople) suffer the permanent oppression and exploitation typical for strategic reasons for the well-being of

their soul. Still, sometimes they revolt under the standard of a revolutionary interpretation of religion - neither rationalizing scholasticism nor straightforward submission to formal rites.(6)

It is crucial to point out the notion that Christianity and Islam inherited Hellenistic scholasticism, i.e., the search for universalism or absolute truths. They also had the added dimension of serving as vehicles for social change through the reorganization of society and attempted to provide happiness on earth through equality, justice, and social solidarity. But in the Greek world, as we shall see with Europe, religion is a secular phenomenon which served the purpose of justifying and spreading Greco-Roman culture and Neoplatonic ideas. Westernized Christianity becomes a vehicle of oppression as opposed to a vehicle for social change. The church became an instrument that sanctified the spreading of the empire in the name of God. No sooner than the Roman Emperor Constantine's conversion to Christianity, the Roman army waited to continue its persecution of Christian converts who had settled in occupied Northern Africa territories. Rome then pursued the de-radicalization of Christianity as a mouthpiece for change was made possible by detaching it from its cultural context and attaching it to the political desires of the spreading Roman Civilization.

Europe would later liberate itself from the domination of metaphysics and focusing more on the "general laws" of nature through the appearance of Islamic-Hellenistic scholasticism as it acquainted them with Ancient concepts.

Migrants from Northern Africa and various parts of the Arab world acculturated southern Europe. Western scholasticism takes its form from the Christian-Islamic-Hellenistic metaphysical construct. The Renaissance also developed out of a dialogue between Islamic philosophy and Caucasian intellectualism and serves as a tool for the West to liberate itself from the domination of a morality-oriented metaphysics and assisted in producing a more materialist philosophy of nature. But also, the outcome is the exchange of ideas between the East and West, with the West getting the better end of the deal. In addition, Europe attempts to trash the primacy of Kemet (Egypt) mainly because of the difficulty of the race question as well as the desire to conquer China and Africa. As a result, it begins to promote a Graeco-Roman- centering of Eurasian history. Earlier, we said that the dividing line in Eurasian intellectualism is the disagreement of scholars over this issue. But like now, mainstream Caucasians, like the Greeks of Alexander, and the Romans of Julius Caesar, recognized the ability to use religion and culture to conquer the world. Afterward, the foundations of a capitalist system are laid, and the East would fall under the domain of Western imperialism.

> The Turkish defeats of the 1680s and the general acceptance of Newtonian physics transformed Europe's self-image. In the post-Newtonian world, writers like Montesquieu, whose reference to the Nykemet (Egyptians) as the greatest philosophers has been noted above, began to contrast Oriental "wisdom" with the "natural philosophy" of Europe. Montesquieu wrote this in 1721; as the century continued, the notion of Caucasian Superiority increased with Caucasian economic and industrial

progress and expansion into other continents. (7)

The structure of Caucasian society allowed the fathers of capitalism to see the power in a new mode of production and its "conquering dynamism". The result was ethnocentrism that embraced the absolute superiority of the Eurasian model. Every aspect of society, from religion to economics, absorbed the ethnocentric overtones that exemplify the Eurasian-centric position. Hence, we uncover how the Westernization use of Christianity is to be understood.

Christianity has always been a tool of Eurasian imperialism to the benefit of an elite class of Eurasians worldwide. It never crystallized into a motivating force that could promote social morality. The Caucasian church, in its secular position, promoted the justification of "Caucasian" superiority and promoted it for practical purposes as a universal prerequisite. The Caucasian way became unquestionably the right way, and the Caucasian model became the basis for the reconstruction of human history. This process would necessarily validate the claims of superiority.

Thereafter, Eurasian began to spread his boundaries and subjugate the people of other lands. As Eurasia spread, capitalism began to crystallize, creating:

> fully developed centers and peripheries incapable of closing the ever-widening gap, making this contradiction within "actually existing" capitalism – a contradiction insurmountable within the framework of the capitalist system -the major and most explosive contradiction of our time.(8)

At this juncture, the Caucasian model becomes anti universalist since it "refuses to use the world as a unit of analysis." The metaphysical quest for universal sameness becomes repugnant to the scientific minds of Europe, and religion continues to serve the sole purpose of justifying social conditions. As a result, the mythical relationship between the West and the Ancient world needs to be exposed. The Caucasian model does not seek true universality. It attempts instead to make the Caucasian model itself universal through the reconstruction of human history.

However, the model itself is foundation-less, being the result of a complete fabrication. It is also unscientific within its own paradigm. Only after World War II did Europe achieve a synthesis between culture, ideology, and society. Adolph Hitler exposed for the world the inner realms of the Caucasian orientation to reality.

Consequently, it has clearly demonstrated itself as one that is uniquely and falsely racist. This exposure leads to a new social reality in Europe: oneness amongst Caucasians. It cannot be overstated that Europe attempted to separate its history and culture to grant itself uniqueness in terms of the rest of humanity.

All other societies were considered backward and undeveloped, never contributing anything to civilization even before Hitler. Europe assumed the duty (in the name of humanity) of forcing these "monstrous and backward" societies into eniyan history by imposing the Caucasian model of society. What solidifies in the culture is the self-prescribed right of Europe to represent human advancement. What Hitler did was to bring back to Europe the same race-oriented imperialism that Europe had taken elsewhere. For the first time, the AfRaKan world was awakened to the necessity of delinking itself from Asiatic-centrism both in terms of intellectualism and economics. Hitler weakened the economic centers of Eurasia. But he might have caused the need for a globally oriented economic and political structure that would become centered through the US and enacted by the League of Nations. To accomplish such a goal, the world powers dictated an impasse:

> In imposing itself on a worldwide scale, capitalism, born in Europe, created a demand for universalism as much at the level of scientific analysis of society as at the level of elaboration of human projects capable of transcending historical limits. (9)

Section 1

REVIEWING THE PROGRESSION
OF A MATERIALIST
METAPHYSICS

Most scholars mistakenly concluded that a demand for a universalism can be obtained through the implementation of socialism. Their mistake was in trying to separate Marxism from Asiatic-centrism of which it is a dimension. Marx converted a lot of followers to the fundamental principles of historical materialism, and they were convinced that socialism would enable humanity to transcend capitalism.

As a result, they stretched the Marxist analysis to the peripheral form of the tributary mode to suggest that Caucasian feudalism is an extension of this form. However, this is a fatal mistake that can only be understood if we return to the idea that Europe insists that it shares with the ancient Greek world. A microscopic investigation shows that what we see developing in Greek philosophy is actually something that plagued Caucasian thought; the often referred to mind/body split.(10) Yet the split does not characterize the thought of non-Greek and non-Caucasian societies. In this respect, in reference to various AfRaKan and Asian metaphysical systems, e.g., the Greeks and Caucasians share a commonality. Maybe not as far as culture and biology are concerned, but certainly in terms of their metaphysical worldview. Europe, who saw himself as having the option of dealing with the morality-oriented Hermeticism on the one hand and the materialism of Hellenism on the other, opted for Hellenism for imperialistic reasons.

But even more profound is the thought that the Greeks could have been Caucasian or the cause of it in this respect. The Greeks intercepted Nykemt (Egyptian) ideas in broken form as they left Kemet (Egypt) and were related to the Greek world through various sources. As George James puts it

> The Athenians sentenced Socrates to death and subsequently caused Plato and Aristotle to flee for their lives from Athens because philosophy was something foreign and unknown to them. For this same reason, we would expect either the Ionians or the Italians to exert their prior claim to philosophy since it made contact with them long before it did with the Athenians, who were always its (philosophy's) greatest enemies, until Alexander's conquest of Egypt, which provided for Aristotle free access to the

library of Alexandria. The Ionians and Italians made no attempt to claim the authorship of philosophy because they were well aware that the Egyptians were the true authors.(11)

Aristotle's overt Greek centering in the Nichomachean Ethics, Metaphysics, and Politics is very different from Plato's Timaeus, Gorgias, and The Republic in terms of centering. Plato's constant references to the Kemety Netcher of wisdom 'Djehuti' seems to play a major role in his philosophy. Moreso, Plato seems to have been very familiar with various NyKemety (Egyptian) doctrines, including the doctrine of "KA" or immortality of the soul and on the creation of the Universe. (12) Herodotus argued that the Greeks had adopted all of their Gods from the Kemety Netcherew.(13) Although Aristotle demonstrates a sense of respect for the Kemety in the arts, he also appears as a Greek nationalist. The twist is that Aristotle's nationalism seems to want to assert the superiority of Greek culture and thought due to its geographical location.

The primary emphasis of the Nichomachean Ethics, which in simple terms is the definition of the highest excellence through the investigation of the nature of causality, allows Aristotle to assert a criterion for moral action. Hence what we discover in the Nichomachean Ethics is the practical application of reason. But, Aristotle is also separating himself from the previous Greek thinkers, especially Plato and Socrates, by trying to create a Greek centering in dealing with particulars instead of universals. The consequence is that Aristotelian thought is more materialistic and more Greek-centered than Platonic thought. Plato seems to be more concerned with establishing abstract forms of justice and truth, whereas Aristotle seems to be preoccupied with causality and its implications on social organization.

If James' claims are true, access to various material from the libraries of Kemet probably resulted in less clarity as to their meanings if the material was analyzed in portions with the help of translators under pressure. It is. not surprising then that since Caucasian culture views Aristotle as one of its founding intellectual "fathers," it has produced so much confusion. While racist scholars have benefitted greatly from these ideas, the average feminist is probably outraged.

Aristotle thought that all things aim naturally, through deliberation at excellence, i.e., all things seek the highest good. We find that Aristotle's concept of man has choices which are influenced by pleasures and pains since his concept wishes to maximize pleasure and minimize pain in every situation. Aristotle believes that these characteristics are external to the nature of his concept and thereby suggested that a temperate and just concept has the potential to learn to control his vices. As activity of thought, contemplation becomes the only activity that is identified as being continuous and pleasurable by nature. However, the problem is that in this being's concept, this activity only consumes part of his life because this concept cannot exist in the world as a mere contemplator without having to entertain some kind of interruption or another. One aspect of this concept's nature, specifically the aspect composed of desire, causes this concept to seek relief or replenishment. In part, the focus of consciousness is externally directed at lesser activities like sex and obtaining wealth and power.

Suggesting that many can derive pleasures from things that have harmful results for others, like stealing and killing. In the inability to maintain these pleasures, the continent man, who is a fully rational agent, initiates the search for a higher good.

> It seems clear that neither is pleasure the good nor is all pleasure desirable, and some pleasures are desirable in themselves while others differ in kind or in their sources. (14)

Aristotle concludes that his concept's pleasures are incomplete and inconsistent. Therefore, whatever the ultimate good is, it is something which is good and pleasurable in itself. It cannot come into being or cease to be through motion. If it moves or ceases to move, this is moving away from itself and would suggest that it is also incomplete. As a result of Aristotle's analysis, we are led to believe that contemplation, ipso facto, is the activity that is good and pleasurable in itself. It is the most continuous activity in the eniyan faculty. And since it allows us to think divine and noble thoughts, it is the most rewarding and has happiness as its final goal.

Contemplation is an internal activity that is pleasurable without external things, and it is self-sufficient and aims at nothing but itself.

For Aristotle, contemplation is:

> superior to our composite nature and is that which is the exercise of the other kinds of excellences."(15)

Each thing has by its nature the best and most pleasurable activity, and for this concept it is intellect and a life devoted jointly to the moral and theoretical excellences. Unlike the planets, for example, which Aristotle believes encounters no alterations and simply moves in circles to their proper places in the universe:

Aristotle's being has to deal with the hindrances that's encountered in everyday life. This is the actuality of this concept's existence and requires a devotion, to some degree, to contemplation. His being must try real hard to achieve a virtuous character because here, the goal is to be able to maximize the use of his practical intelligence. Then his only desire is to accomplish that which is good in and of itself: contemplation.

The benefit of having a character that is virtuous is the discovery of happiness. Contemplation allows him to reflect on the higher aspect of his being and gives him the ability to imitate and approximate divine, and considered like "theos" like because it surpasses the living body, a thing which is driven by emotions and sensations. It becomes then the best quality in humans, which reflects the mortality of human existence, being that humans have to be mindful of human affairs.

The virtuous eniyan sees that what appears good and what is good for him is the same thing. Therefore, eniyan is able to detect the truth in all his actions through rationalization. However, his human characteristics still make him susceptible to the weakness of fallacy, and eniyan is unable to detach himself from the world in which eniyan finds himself. This being desires excellence but cannot devote himself to complete contemplation. Aristotle says that:

> The excellences of the faculty of nutrition and growth are not even human excellences; for in so far as one is a being, there must be present reasoning as

a governing element and action and
reasoning governs not reasoning but
desires and passions, where it is
necessary that one have these parts. (17)

Aristotle is suggesting nature has given this
being a mind and desires, which allows him to
be both an intellectual and emotional being.
Again, this being believes that his intellectual
aspect of eniyan supersedes the other. It
provides this being with freedom and self-
sufficiency. The emotions throw this bring into
a world of pain where the desire for pleasure is
his only recourse. Eniyan's actions reflect the
conflict between what oun has deliberated as
being right or wrong and the way oun acts.
They prove that oun finds himself acting
against his own knowledge of the truth. Oun
will power is constantly being overtaken by the
appetite of the body.

Contemplation for Aristotle represents the
divine elements in his being, and it allows him
to contemplate the truth continuously. The truth
is divine, and oun who reflects the truth seeks
excellence and is also divine.

But such a life [bios] is too exalted to suit
a human being.   It is not qua human that

one lives in this way but insofar as there is something godlike in one. And the active exercise of the other sort of excellence by as much as it surpasses the compound [to suntheton, viz. the living body possessed of emotions, sensations, e.t.c.].(18)

It is flourishing for the eniyan character to have complete knowledge of the true self, the intellectual self. In Aristotle's words, the "god-like man" cherishes the good that is recognized in his own nature. Aristotle's "man" contemplates himself to be excellent and divine. This being is not motivated by pleasures and pains since this being sees his own activities as making him happy.

The final cause then produces motion as being loved, and by what is moved, it moves other things. The unmoved mover then is of necessity being; and insofar as it is by necessity, its mode of being is suitable, and in this way, it is a first principle.(19)

The Demiurge, or that which is able to contemplate itself only, is the highest good and the object of pure happiness. Thus the role of the Nichomachean Ethics was to describe the cause of pure contemplation and how it moves mankind to a higher level of happiness. The true nature of man compels him to be a contemplator; however, the forces of society have him caught up in a dualistic world where he is distracted by the forces of everyday events.

Yet, "Man" is not an emotional or sensual being by nature for Aristotle. "Man" moves like all things toward the final eternal cause, which is the Demiurge or pure happiness. At the same time, the Demiurge or unmoved mover is the cause of all motion in the universe. All the particular things have a movement caused by it. In connection with Aristotle's other ideas of continent and incontinence, potentiality and actuality, as well as causality, oun definitely seems to have believed that individuals, e.g., have particular functions in society. Some awon Okunrin are moved to lead over others, as some awon Okunrin are moved/fit to be slaves, while others have the potential to be masters. Here's another citation:

For example, the union of male and female is essential for reproduction; and this is not a matter of choice, but is due to the natural urge, which exists in the other animals too and in plants, to propagate one's kind. Equally essential is the combination of the natural ruler and ruled for the purpose of preservation. For the element that can use its intelligence to look ahead is by nature ruler and by nature master, while that which has the bodily strength to do the actual work is by nature a slave, one of those who are ruled. (20)

The search for a universal culture reflected through some type of social organization seems to be an essential aspect of Aristotelian thought. However, as Amin pointed out, the Greek innovation in human thought resulted in the birth of materialist metaphysics. Universalism is not a physical or a material reality and, therefore, not a material possibility. This explains why Eurasian-centric metaphysics cannot account for the spiritual dimension of an AfRaKan metaphysical system. In other words, the contribution which Kemet and the Chaldeans civilizations (the AfRaKan world) gave to Hellenistic philosophy was a spiritual and not material one. Early on, Plato seems to be promoting Justice, Temperance, and Wisdom as versions of MAAT and Rhetoric in order to promote the practice of self-knowledge and fine-tuning of the soul. The Kemety asserted that the world was made up of complementary parts as opposed to the opposites espoused by a mind/body philosophy. The persistence in the modern world to classify Kemet as "Occidental" or "Semitic", while disconnecting from its AfRaKan heritage, and both are disconnected from their AfRaKan Mut Netcherew Neteru, making the rest of AfRaKa the "insignificant others" of world civilization, has caused the inability in understanding Ancient Kemet fully. In jumping from forms to categories, Greek thought moves a step further to adopt the materialism of transcendence. Whereas Plato probably attempted to teach a liberal morality-oriented philosophy, Aristotle moves in the direction of the Arts and Sciences as well as a criterion for objectivity. Therefore, the idea of the immortality of the soul in AfRaKan thought as well as Platonic thought, should not appear to have simply fallen into the Greek world. It is a reflection of a conscious eniyan activity that attempts to understand life, themselves, and their relation to the universe and its happenings. The idea reflects in all arenas of AfRaKan culture, which supports the possibility that even if it did fall out of the sky, it fell in relation to other AfRaKan events, and its meaning was derived and explained in the form of AfRaKan conclusions to formulate AfRaKan cultures.

In Nykemet (Egyptian) architecture, temples reflect the symbolic correspondence between the movement of the life forces through the body. The corridors of a particular structure would represent the path of nerves that carry the life force to the various locations of the body for different purposes. Behind the Egyptian approach was the importance of self-understanding. Knowledge of the body which symbolically is like a temple, allows consciousness to free itself from the bodily fetters that attempt to trap the life force. (21) The body is seen as a temporary carrier for the soul and not as a permanent cage. Also, like a temple, the body has various doors through which invocation liberates the soul. Each door is represented by a principle/spirit and where their importance is honored.

Since the body is only the temporary capsule of the soul when it decays, the soul is guided by the principle/spirits to its immortal primordial state. Therefore, consciousness of the body represents a portion of the full arena of consciousness. The mind/body consciousness promotes either body or mind, and the symbolic consciousness promotes harmony between the two and the transcendence of either.

Especially since the Kemety were concerned with developing the human faculties to their fullest capabilities. Okunrin was seen as a symbolic representation of the powers of the universe and has the ability to gain consciousness of these powers. Hence, eniyan development of consciousness becomes the primary concern of Ancient AfRaKan systems of religion/theology of which philosophy is a branch.

Section 2

USING BUDDHISM TO DEMONSTRATE THE ETHNOCENTRISM IN HEGELIAN THOUGHT

For the most part, Caucasian methods have inherited the materialism of the Greeks. They have also been dominated by false notions of universality, objectivity, and absolute "truth". An AfRaKan centered method must refrain from denying the relevance of a Caucasian analysis for Caucasians. However, it must also outline how these same notions surfaced at a time when Europe was attempting to promote the model of its own superiority and created myths about the rest of the world's people. One of the myths was the Caucasian claim of all "progressive" human activity along with the association of "backwardness" to other peoples. The claim to superiority has been a central and persistent theme in Caucasian discourses. According to Preiswork and Perrot:

> There is projection, upon cultures other than Western, of a system of values common to the whole of the western world. Thus, for example, in their relations with AfRaKan, Asian and Indian American cultures, Westerners, whether representative of a free market economy or a planned economy, act on the basis of fairly similar conceptions of time, work, productivity. (22)

The West has been unable to develop a method that, when employed, acknowledges the importance of non-Western values, which is a result of the natural Caucasian right to prioritize Europe in relation to all events under analysis. As reflected in cross-cultural encounters, the West has not maintained its own ideal of neutrality through objectivity.

The Lutheran Reformation did not extend the same type of consideration to non-Caucasian and their culture during the spread of Caucasian imperialism. For instance, in its perspectives on other peoples, we can always find dehumanizing conclusions. Its greatest thinkers have been known to uphold some of the most racist positions and applied them in their analyses and writings on other people. What surfaced in the interim is a psychological mishap, a culture of racist myth-making. Because of the contact between Asia and Europe during the 17th and 18th century, one would think that a genuinely effective comparison between Hegel's Phenomenology of Spirit and Buddhism would have occurred. Nevertheless, Hegel had a perjorative ranking for other non-Caucasian cultures. Consciousness is a central theme in Hegelian and Buddhist thought. It is possible that the hegemony in Western culture and the preoccupation with keeping Greece as the foundation of Caucasian civilization caused him to be ignorant of alternative viewpoints. Any given Caucasian philosopher could lecture on the necessity of human liberty in the morning and on the justification of slavery and colonialism in the evening.

It is possible to continuously demonstrate the racist remarks in the position of various Caucasian thinkers. Yet, the structure of Caucasian thought presents suitable evidence to demonstrate the type of mentality that produced these remarks a posteriori. We are therefore obliged to articulate the belief that Caucasian metaphysics is not only strictly materialist in orientation but also one-dimensionally hegemonic. The idea of transcendence surfaces again as we encounter an understanding of consciousness in Hegel and in Buddhism. Immediately there are intriguing parallels. At the same time, indirectly, the Buddhist offers a surprising alternative that could possibly serve as the basis for analyzing Hegel's critique of consciousness.

What one could conclude from this section is that I am comparing Hegel's idea of a possible synthesis in consciousness through the recognition of Geist with the idea of the void or emptiness in Buddhism. Buddhism, as an example, shows exactly how Europe perpetuated the materialism that it inherited from Greece. This is because I believe that Hegel's absolute mind is taken a step further by the Buddhist concept of Nirvana. Even though Hegel's deals with subject/object synthesis, it still does not escape the mind/body conflict. Hegel's critique of Skepticism and Skepticism is incomplete given that Hegel limits himself with a mind that is unable to ascend the existence of "Notions" in thought. Hegel's absolute mind does not suggest the in differentiation in thought that we find in Buddhism.

After inheriting the moral aspirations of the Enlightenment, and the freedom attained from the Greek pursuit of reason, Georg Hegel sought to refute the external authority held by the established church and the hierarchies of command to restore eniyan's autonomy in a Caucasian based society.

His objective was to return wholeness and expressive unity between eniyan and nature and eniyan to eda eniyan. Therefore, his philosophy is supposed to meet the demands of expressive unity and reason in order to liberate eniyan from the deadness of the authoritarianism which he detected in his contemporaries. At the time, the supernatural claims of the church were said to be unquestionable. So to denounce this external control over the minds of eda eniyan, Hegel saw his efforts as a regeneration of the Enlightenment, the best of Greek spirit, with the ideals of Christianity within it.

As a matter of fact,

> The regeneration he (Hegel) looks for is one in which men archive the freedom of moral self-determination, while at the same time recovering wholeness or integrity where reason is not at odds with the passions, or spirit with sensibility, but where the whole man is moved spontaneously to moral goodness. (23)

Hegel wishes to unite reason with sensibility in order to end the domination that exists between eniyan and nature. Therefore, the synthesis between reason and sensibility should liberate eniyan from a preoccupation with domination through an extinction of opposition.

> This was the original wrench which created the unhappy consciousness as Hegel will call it later, the consciousness of separation from nature, a consciousness in which unity and mutuality are replaced by domination and servitude, between eniyam and nature, nature and spirit, and ultimately also a consequence, between man and man. For Hegel as one who held to the aspiration of expressive unity, this consciousness could not but be unhappy, a tearing asunder.(24)

Oun concludes here that the dichotomies which have surfaced between eniyan and nature, object and subject, are the result of a forged and unnatural separation between the two entities. At the same time, oun wants to show that the necessity of freedom produced the separation between eniyan and nature by driving the two forces into tragic conflict. However, out of the same necessity, a higher reconciliation is made possible, and the idea of Geist and its movement provides the final synthesis towards this realization.   Geist is supposed to offer "one-ness" in all things.(25) It posits all things as finite beings in which Geist manifests itself. Geist is the infinite whole, whereas eniyan is the finite "Geist medium" being, in relation to the relative movement of a Geist as a whole. It synthesizes man's spirit by uniting the separateness and expensive unity with the spirit of nature.

> As a consequence, freedom dissolves this union. The oppositions are those which arise from the breaking up of the original expressive unity. (26)

> As eniyan progresses, oun begins to understand or relate to nature in brutal terms. Hegel argues that this opposition counteracts the purpose of knowing. The opposition begins to posit things as outside of the reach of the mind. (27)

> Therefore, a sort of complex develops where individual freedom is asserted over integral freedom. In order to be free, each eniyan must become her/his own master to demand recognition. Nevertheless, Hegel has no problem with separateness as long as it is seen within the context of

integrated freedom where the individual exist in a larger social whole. On the other foot, the inability to identify with an integrated freedom produces self-consciousness, which leads to self-dependence, autonomy, and opposition. Consciousness becomes trapped in dichotomy and ambiguity.

An identity arises which, after being unable to sustain itself on its own produces opposition. The self posits an identity and a difference in relation to the other "self". 28

It also begins to realize a certain form which Hagel speaks of a self-realization. This is consciousness attempting to position itself as finite.

Hence for consciousness to be located, it must be somewhere, sometime. But if a consciousness is somewhere, sometime, it is not somewhere else, sometime else. It thus has a limit between itself and what is not itself. It is finite. (29)

Consciousness becomes bipolar, requiring the distinction between itself and others, and produces subjects and objects. Also, it is here that Geist comes to full self awareness by successfully shaping its vehicle into a complete expression of itself. The finite self is posited in the larger context of Geist. Things by themselves are contradictory, and the contradictory cannot exist on its own. Geist brings them into infinitude by synthesizing them with the absolute. At this point, the distinction or opposition within consciousness terminates.

> Every partial reality is posited by the whole or absolute as a necessary condition of this absolute's existence· for this absolute can only be as embodied in a world of external, physical things and finite spirits. Yet, these partial realities, just because they exist externally, each alongside the others, make a standing claim to independence which belies their status as posited vehicles of the whole. (30)

It follows that contradictions arise by identifying things by the external, which posits them. Self-certainty, therefore, is what produces the contradiction in consciousness.

We enter now into Hegel's critique of consciousness, which he entitles "freedom from self-consciousness"· The critique of Stoicism and Skepticism attempts to project consciousness as being dual-natured. It extends from the dialectic of the Master/Slave relationship. Hegel suggests that men achieve integrity through recognition and when recognition is not accomplished mutually through reciprocation, conflict, and contradiction arises. Moreso, a struggle proceeds as one group attempts to dominate another group in order to demand recognition. Thus the group which makes the demands becomes the master, and the group which succumbs to the demands, becomes the slaves. At the same time, one surfaces as a consumer and the other as a laborer.

For Hegel, the relationship is maintained by a fear of death in the heart of the slave. His inability to deal with an external world over which he has no control pushes him to his only refuge; inner thought. Labor and inner thought enable the slave to become conscious of a universal freedom.

Oun grasps the power to transform things through his thought usage, and oun realizes that everything that oun creates results from his own reflection as a universal thinking being and then materializes his thoughts into objects. The slave sees himself as a creator. However, oun is still bonded by a world that is dominated by his masters, and death is the tool that masters use to keep him in his position. The slave recognizes that obtaining his freedom necessarily means an inevitable confrontation with death.

> The return to the universal Geist involves an overcoming of the particular external existence in which it is embodied. This is why as we have seen, death comes necessarily to living things. Of course, the highest negation of his external existence is achieved by man in thought, that is, while still alive. But he is helped to this inner negation by coming face to face with death, the final outer negation, for this shows the true status of all the

external particularity in his life, it shows it as necessarily passing, as destined to be negated, and thus invites the negation in thought which is the return to the universe.(31)

The Stoic comes to a higher level of self-realization through what Hegel calls universal reflection by positing differences in the pure movement of thought where consciousness knows itself as the essence in "being in itself", i.e., as a universal mode of being. Importance is taking away from the specific things and placed on the different Notions or different thoughts. The Stoic seeks freedom in the pure universality of thought. Free thought is pure thought and lacks a criterion of truth. It sees itself as being true. Consciousness destroys content and becomes only the Notions in thought. Thought at this level is said to be "contentless", having no content. This leads Hegel to suggest that Skepticism is the realization of what Stoicism was merely the notion. The Skeptic gives thought to the content that Stoicism denies. Therefore, consciousness is unhappy, being forced to recognize its dual nature, consisting of both

Notion and content. The consequence is unhappy consciousness.

The idea of "contentless" thought is also present in Buddhism. However, the Buddhist takes Hegel's critique of Stoicism to a higher level. In fact, they state that consciousness can achieve a state of Un-differentiating and undiscriminating thought which would mean an end to Hegel's Notions in Stoicism. The aim of Buddhism is achieved in a state of consciousness where the mind experiences undiscriminating emptiness in thought. This achievement is referred to as Nirvana which is, in retrospect, the attainment of the Absolute Mind and spiritual perfection.

What is produced is a state of mind where an individual has gained perfect wisdom and is totally unconscious of pain and suffering. The idea is that these qualities are effects of a discriminating consciousness or mind.

Buddhism attempts to direct consciousness towards the absolute by blowing out the flame, which fuels the process of becoming. Hence its moral and spiritual codes utilize a follower's existence as a dialectical vehicle in order to aim him towards Nirvana.

The end result is not a synthesis between subject and object but a denial of both as distinguishable. For Buddhist views reality as emptiness.

Buddhism teaches that there is nothing about a sentient or transitory being that can be considered as permanent. In fact, all beings that are born begin to age, become ill, and die. Thus the Buddhist concludes that all things are in a constant state of flux and are always becoming. There is nothing permanent within beings like a fixated "soul". All things within the Buddhist doctrine are impermanent—suffering or dukkha results in the inability to disconnect consciousness from the process of life. Life consists of stages of suffering, i.e., birth and death. Even pleasures produce suffering in the sense that pleasures are not eternal. The consciousness of self-identity is the same as a consciousness of an insidious entity. Therefore, we can detect the description of life in the Four Noble Truths: 1). The truth of Dukkha (suffering) ;2)the truth of the arising of Dukkha; 3)the truth of the cessation of Dukkha; and 4)the truth of the path which leads to the cessation of Dukkha.

The Buddhist doctrine asserts that all things fit somehow into component parts, and these can be seen as form and matter (rupa), sensations, perceptions, psychic dispositions or constructions, and conscious thoughts.

> As the arising and decaying moments of matter, sensations, perceptions, and consciousness interact, they create a residue of energy reservoir termed mental formations, which condition or occasion the continued arising and decaying of the aggregates. (32)

Consequently, everything is changing within the sentient being. Therefore, the nature of the self is a ceaseless striving to fulfill desires, and these desires are linked to a cycle on the wheel of becoming. An attachment with the self produces a covetous thinking mind and the desire to fulfill selfish needs. As the mind and body interact, the contact gives rise to sensations and desires.

Consciousness then is consciousness of a self-perpetuating self and produces unrealistic and self-centered behavior.

All living things continue a cycle of rebirth until they are able to escape suffering by blowing out the flame of craving. To escape, one must detach consciousness from the misleading identification with the self. The purpose of meditation aims at the specific goal of achieving this task. It leads sentient beings towards a higher state of consciousness where the mind is able to free itself from the craving of the body. The goal is Nirvana, a state absent of greed, hatred, and delusion, i.e., absent of self-identity and discrimination. The Buddha's dialectic, as we said earlier, utilizes life as a practical manifestation of a pathway towards the higher consciousness of the Void.

Emptiness Reality or the void alone represents oun changeless reality. The dialectical process by which this Emptiness Reality or the void alone represents the changeless. The dialectical process by which this ultimate truth is reached is known as the Middle Path of Eightfold Negations, which systematically denies all antithetical assertions regarding things: "there is no production, no extinction, no annihilation no permanence, no unity, no diversity, no coming in, no going out. Production, extinction, etc, are proved by the school to be unreal by the use of the Four Points of Argument", that is, by refuting an idea as neither being nor non-being as being is, by refuting an idea as being, as non-being, as both being and non-being, and as neither being nor non-being. The belief in any of the four is an extreme and must be transcended by a higher synthesis through the dialectic method until the Ultimate Void is arrived at which is the Absolute Middle. (33)

For the Buddhists, consciousness or the mind has two characteristics: the enlightened and the unenlightened. The unenlightened mind activates the subjective consciousness and clings to the world of unreal objects. It attaches itself to the phenomenon and produces distinctions between itself and others. It cherishes its own existence and thereby causes a split between the original undifferentiated unity into two components; the mind and the world of objects. On the other hand, the enlightened mind is led to Higher and Common Truths, which can be seen as a oneness in all things.

The dialectic has now reached a state of voidness where there appears no content and no distinction. Consciousness has gained control over desires and, in the process, attained absolute wisdom. The Buddhist monk develops what is labeled "mindfulness".

> The eight principles can be summarized into three essential directing fundamentals: to raise the morality to a prescribed minim, to develop the power of concentration to one-pointedness of the mind, and to gain insight into the ultimate realities of nature within oneself. Buddhism offers a strict ethical and disciplinary code in order to develop an insightful method of understanding. It pushes consciousness towards an abode through the use of righteousness and spiritual perfection, which it prescribes in its dialectic. Unlike the misconception made by most Western versions of Christianity, the Buddhist heaven, Nirvana, is attainable as a compliment to life. Consciousness experiences perfect wisdom. (34)

Where the Buddhist take Hegel's critique of Stoicism and consciousness to a higher level is in their suggestion of voidness in thought where thought itself is empty of content and of Notions. The Buddhist suggest that even Notions are content to the Absolute mind since the mind is capable of being undiscriminating.

> Rightly conceived, it (nirvana) is one in which the particularities of ordinary experience and the illusory distinctions of the discriminating mind are left behind, and the religious aspect of this is that it is a state which compassionate oneness with others has transcended all thoughts oneself as a separately distinguishable entity. Nothing is outside of Nirvan. (35)

Hegel's critique of Stoicism and Skepticism leads him to suggest the "Unhappy Consciousness"· But this is because oun suggests that the Stoic reflects only with Notions and is unable to give content to reality. Therefore, his Geist offers a synthesis between idea and content being that they are reflections of the expressive unity in the spirit of Geist and are said to be one. The Buddhist argues that there cannot be a split in something unreal, and the only synthesis necessary is to lead consciousness toward Emptiness. For Hegel, when the Stoic recognizes the universality of pure thought, oun engages in thought without content. However, the Stoic is an idealist since oun utilizes the notions of ideals, e.g., Truth, Justice, Freedom, e.t.c.These are qualities that are given content after a reflective interaction with the world of experience.

The difference is that the Buddhist absolute mind is undiscriminating and void of content where Hegel's absolute mind is full and reflective. The Buddhists offer an attempt to elevate consciousness beyond the movement of pure thought by penetrating the ideas of Notion and discrimination and to promote the discovery of Voidness or emptiness within all things. The distinction between what could be labeled as content and what could be labeled as material is not a clear and distinguishable subject in Hegel. However, Buddhism is more clear that content is material and material content simply because the forces of the universe have the power to materialize. In Christianity, "God" has the power to actualize his words. Eniyan is the actualization of the word of God for example. Power in these

Religious concepts that transcendence, i.e., the ability to move beyond, escapes the confines of a mind/body and physical material conflict. (36)

Section 3

MARXISM AND THE SOLIDIFICATION OF MATERIALISM

Karl Marx also embraces a strictly materialistic conception of the universe. His analysis is a classic example of the problem of trying to divide Caucasian concepts and conclusions from their Caucasian metaphysical groundings. A critique of colonialism successfully demonstrates the impossibility of such a gesture. In doing so, we expose an element in Marxism that most so-called AfRaKan Socialist thinkers have attempted to ignore. This is not meant with any hostility, but the abolishment of an AfRaKan centered methodology has brought us to the moment where we must review the significance of foreign tools and ideologies in Africa.(37) In fact, it can be said that the distortion of Karl Marx, as the liberator of the oppressed, has confused many intellectuals in promoting Marxism throughout the AfRaKan and Asian world. Marxism has surfaced as the center point of their methodologies and critiques. Socialism, in its AfRaKan manifestation, has become Africa's so-called savior.

For instance, this seems to have been the view of Joseph Nyrere, a prominent Socialist leader in Africa, regarding the question of equality in Africa:

> Although we try to hide the fact, and despite the exaggeration which our critics have frequently indulged in, it is true that the women in traditional society were regarded as having a place in the community which was not only different but was also, to some extent inferior. It is impossible to deny that the women did, and still do, more than their share of the works in the fields and in the homes. By virtue of their sexual orientation, they suffered from inequalities that had nothing to do with their contribution to the family welfare. Although it is wrong to suggest that they have always been an oppressed group, it is true that ill-treatment and enforced subservience could be there a lot within traditional society. This is certainly inconsistent without a socialist conception of equality and the right of all human beings, and the right of all to live in such security and is

consistent with equal security and
freedom for all.(38)

This seems to suggest that traditional AfRaKan
society had no place for women. The role of
obinrin in traditional Africa has a context from
which it should be viewed. AfRaKan salvation
exists in the same context. Unfortunately,
though, AfRaKan thinkers fail to recognize the
tragedy of equivocating AfRaKan salvation
with Socialism. The tragedy is that in
accepting Marx's prism, it is like looking at
AFRaKa with Caucasian eyes. Historical
materialism "ontologies" the Caucasian
experience and makes it historically superior to
non-Caucasian societies. Marx's conclusions
were definitely influenced by the idea of
progress and the movement of Hegel's Geist
from east to west. Tsenay Serequerbehan
accuses AfRaKan thinkers of not being critical
of Marxism in this dimension. Oun suggests
that AfRaKan thinkers:

> have all fallen short of a systematic and
> critical undoing of the Caucasian
> metaphysics that structures and grounds
> Marx's perspective. (39)

In the article, "Karl Marx and African Emancipatory Thought: A critique of Marx's Caucasian Metaphysics," Tsenay regards the task of a systematic de-structuring of the metaphysical grounding present in Asiatic-centrism as the negative task of AfRaKan philosophy. Tsenay proposes that other AfRaKan thinkers approach Marxism in a similar fashion to make elements of his analysis useful.

The critique by Tsenay offers another testimony in the ongoing trial of Asiatic-Centrism. In fact, oun elaborates on the adverse effects of Asiatic-centrism and includes Marx's metaphysical grounding. Most scholars only make minor references to this possibility believing that Marx represents a radical change in Caucasian thought. It is believed that Marxism:

> successfully demystifies the fundamental economism of the dominant ideology to such an extent that after Marx, it is no longer possible to think the way people did before him.(40)

However, Tsenay puts us back on track by pointing out that it is much more difficult to "Disentangle" or "unhinge" Marxism from its metaphysical grounding. Marx's materialist conception of history is very much Asiatic interpretation of human existence. Because of his virtual ignorance of non-Caucasian civilizations, Marx supported colonialism. Oun thought that the spreading of Europe:

> Draws all nations, even the most barbarian, into civilization. Furthermore, it cannot be otherwise since the history of human society is the history of class struggles. (41)

Marx's Europe was the model of the highest level of civilization, and his interpretation of history justified the historical necessity of the global expansion of Europe and, thus, capitalism. Oun insisted that capitalism had revealed eniyan's best attempt to dominate the forces of nature by an extremely sophisticated mode of production. In other words, Europe was the scenario in which the most advanced form of class struggle occurred.

Marx projected his construct as a global necessity, maintaining that if humanity was to ever move past class struggle, the proletariat would have to gain control of the state.

As a consequence, we find in Marx, the justification of the Asiatic conquest of other peoples. It is the responsibility of Europe to induce the formation of society around the mode of production, and violence becomes its agent. Thereafter Marx endorses the destruction of the indigenous societies by Caucasian conquest.

> England, it is true, in causing a social revolution in Hindostan, was actuated only by the vilest interests and was stupid in her manner of enforcing them. But that is not the question. The question is, can eniyan fulfill it's destiny without s the unconscious tool of history in bringing out that revolution. The fundamental revolution in the social state of Asia? If not, whatever may have been the crimes of England, she was the unconscious tool of history in bringing about that revolution. (42)

For him, the Asianization of the native is of the utmost importance. It is through the "assimilate" or "evolve" that the non-Caucasian has any hope. Keeping this in mind, it becomes questionable as to whether or not

Marxism can truly emancipate the non-caucasian societies. Mainly because in the context of Marxist thought, the native's struggle is seen only as an adjunct to that of the Asian proletariat and is administered by the asianized native. Disagreeing with Marx, first, we assert that the possibility of emancipation surfaces when the natives reject their assimilation and instead attempt to indigenize themselves with their pre-colonial history and culture. Fanon and Albert Memmi have suggested that the liberation of the colonized comes through the recovery of self or process of self-discovery. Their attempts to make self-discovery a formidable aspect of any decolonization process are useful in understanding the necessity of an AfRacentric Perspective.

> Where a real struggle for freed has taken place, the westernized native is absorbed back into the indigenous milieu and re-integrated into the cultural heritage from

which he had been alienated by asianization and which he now feels as domination. This does not mean that the Caucasian values (Marxist theory, for example) infused in the person of the westernized native are discarded. Rather the arrogant ethnocentrism in which these values are in cases is purged, and Caucasian values and technics are accepted for what they are, and technics are accepted purged, and Caucasian values culturally circumscribed products of human_existence... elements of Caucasian culture are appropriated and become indigenized organic aspects of re-emerging AfRaKaN cultures. (43)

AfRaKan socialist agenda contains the belief that Caucasian values, methods, and technics (like Marxism, or even Capitalism and industrialization) can be AfRaKanized or indigenized by " slightly stretching" the anatomy of Marx's critique. The stretching would include dislocating Marxism from its Caucasian orientation, i.e., its materialist conception of history and its "ontologization" of the Caucasian experience. Marxism can be re-thought and indigenized by excusing his ignorance of the non-Caucasian world. He is justifiably excused of his preoccupation with Europe even though he seems to be completely trapped by it.

Nevertheless, when Marx attempted to look at other societies, it was only too appropriate how these societies could be Caucasianized and made part of the socialist world revolution. What oun called the pre-capitalist world was labeled immature and barbaric. Europe's duty was to force those societies that existed on its periphery to drop their superstitious past and fulfill eniyan's destiny towards maturity and communism.

In summary, Marx becomes a classic example of the fallacy of depending on Europe for Africa's salvation. The utilization of imported "tools" as if they can be detached from their cultural foundations is also a misconception. The reason is that it is incapable of allowing us to contest or destroy the channels of colonialism. A perfect example is how colonialism is equivocated with capitalism, yet socialism, another Caucasian import, is not AfRaKanized. How can either be AfRaKanized when their metaphysical conception is strictly materialistic? Does Africa have a socially constructed reality? The fallacy which most so-called AfRaKan thinkers have committed is to think that Marx was criticizing capitalism, that the voids in Marxism can be filled and a synthesis with certain aspects of AfRaKan culture can be used to critique colonialism; or that Marx offers the only valid critique of capitalism. Marx is critiquing capital as it relates to the working class and the unequal distribution of wealth. However, Marx being inextricably tied to an evolutionist model of history does not see the deformation which causes colonialism from a non-materialist foundation. Marx's critique proceeds after the solidification of the capitalist mode. Our quest is to review capitalism as the necessary byproduct of colonialism and how both have dismantled AfRaKan societies.

CHAPTER III

COLONIALISM AND, AFRAKAN AND AFRAKAN AMERICAN PHILOSOPHY

Is it really possible to draw a distinction between Marxism, colonialism, and capitalism? The AfRaKan world has experienced them all too its detriment. Our Africanity is not reinforced through indigenizing Caucasian values and technics. If we intend to halt the Caucasianization of the AfRaKan, we must first excavate the AfRaKan reality from its distorted subjugation under Europe. There arrives the need for a truly AfRaKan centered critique of capitalism, colonialism, Marxism, or any other "ism" that comes out of the abyss of Asiatic-centrism. Of course, this would include an analysis of the intellectual crisis that AfRaKan thinkers find themselves are in currently. (44)

Serequeberhan wants to appropriate cultural forms of existence which have endured against colonialism and incorporate them with the indigenized or AfRaKanized versions of Eurasian values and technics under the framework of eniyan synthesis. The fallacy in his thinking is that it does not seem to reverse the destruction of the AfRaKan world caused by Asiatic-centrism; rather, it reinforces it. It heightens AfRaKa's forced addiction on Asiatic solutions. We used Marx as an example to show how even socialism when an attempt is made to supposedly AfRaKanize it, which results in the displacement of the AfRaKan. Our position does not simply apply to Marxism but to any other attempts to adopt Caucasian methods as tools.

The process of accepting them forces the AfRaKaN to become more Asiatic in his worldview than AfRaKan. Europe gets prioritized at the displacement of Africa, and Asiatic influences receive more significance over AfRaKan ones. Even if not marginalized, Europe has no stranglehold over the development of solutions to human problems. However, that is not the problem! The problem is, theoretically, AfRaKan intellectuals have feared being disconnected from the umbilical cord of Western notions of reason, science, and objectivity. Therefore, many refuse to consider dropping Europe altogether as a source of intellectual inspiration even though it is conceived that these same Eurocentrism cannot take us past colonialism because its intellectuals could not look beyond the conception of Western history and what they saw as class struggles in the Greek and Roman worlds. Asiatic-centrism is a product of the same events that led to colonialism.

Colonialism

In reference to all serious AfRaKan thinkers, a critique of Marxism via Eurocentrism must come from within an indigenous AfRaKan understanding of reality. Instead of analyzing Marxism, materialism, AfRaKan thinkers have used Marx to critically analyze AfRaKan society. What they are guilty of can be seen as such: they extrapolate a specific characteristic that is indigenous to AfRaKan societies, it is then especially dialectical and historical modified, intensified and equivocated with the Western mode, and then re-injected into their analysis. For example, so-called socialist thinkers extrapolate disputes between ethnicities (called tribal wars by the Western intellectuals) from the context in which they occur, modify them so that they are conceived as class struggles, equivocate it with Marx's materialist conception of history, and re-inject it into their analysis to justify the evolutionary necessity of socialism. Again, the position reflects a strictly materialist conception of reality and asserts that reality is socially constructed.

However, in the same sense that "Western" science has said that lunar and solar motion effect planetary life, AfRaKan traditional knowledge has always maintained a relationship with the lunar, solar, and stellar phenomenon. In other words, reality may have a social aspect, but it is also influenced by cosmic forces, which would mean that society by itself alone does not shape reality or eniyan totally.

> The Dogon speaks of male and a female soul and of pairs of rays. These are indeed principles of opposites -- syzygies of the Hermopolitan cosmogony--which are the basis of the creation of the universe. (45)

For the most part, the disruption of AfRaKan history has not been explicated in terms of indigenous forms of understanding. Colonization has been classified in terms of privileges and disadvantages with the economic disparities. Our main focus is to demonstrate the necessity of returning to the utilization of pre-colonial systems of understanding for explanation in terms of how colonialism disrupted the cycles of life established by the native people's generations before colonialism. The importance of AfRaKan intellectual development becomes manifest in understanding the transgression of forms of existence. At the precise moment that we begin to express the characteristics that make for a unique part of human experience, we escape the current problematics concerning the nature of AfRaKan Philosophy.

However, the current discussions remain necessary to understanding where AfRaKans find themselves in the world. The works of Paulo Freire, Frantz Fanon, and Albert Memmi, all describe colonialism in a similar fashion. They have placed in perspective the complex nature of the colonial relationship that emerges between the colonizer and the colonized, oppressor and the oppressed, and the foreigner and the native. Their efforts deserve much reverence for outlining the process of usurpation and disfranchisement that colonization forces on the indigenous or native peoples. Indeed, their critiques offer very helpful insights on the effects of the colonial structures that are placed in the paths of the colonized. And they have also exposed the interested reader to ambiguities of society by pointing to its colonial injustices and wickedness. The reader is left to conclude that colonialism is a disgraceful incursion on humanity and begins to theorize the possible decolonization of AfRaKa. Consequently, we arrive at a point where we have to figure out how relevant the solutions suggested by these thinkers are too decolonization. Their antidotes are henceforth appraised.

Our efforts toward liberation lead us into an inevitable confrontation with the colonial forces. To destroy them, we must critique them. Moreover, we must decide if we are to critique them within the framework of a colonized people with the mentality that accompanies it or choose to escape its barriers as much as possible. The first option is instantly captured by the second because if we are to escape its barriers, we must develop a critique that does not leave us entrapped in the colonial context, i.e., our efforts must lead us away from those ideologies that lead us back to Europe. Our struggle becomes one of self-directedness, and in order to center its perspective, we must produce an understanding of ourselves that affirms our being and liberates us from the colonial dogmas. To interject an AfRacentric perspective so that a critique of colonialism can be accomplished, we must insure that we carry out our critique in relation to AfRaKan culture and values. At the same time, we must keep in mind that:

> National liberation is the overcoming of the colonialist interruption of the colonized; it is a process of returning to the source out of which the colonized spun themselves into existence prior to being colonized. (46)

> Therefore, it is impossible to critique our situation with much success if we continue to portray ourselves as European constructs in foreign methods and concepts. Our critique inspires a revolution in the way we conceive ourselves, and the end result is an autonomously produced method/ideology/and culture.

Albert Memmi's analysis in The Colonizer and the Colonized submerges into the worlds of both the colonized and the colonizer. He tries with much success to describe the economic setting and its impact on the structures and institutions of a colonized society.

By doing so, he exposes the privileges that colonialism provides the colonizer and the disadvantages it causes the colonized. In Memmi's eyes, the relationship that exists between the colonizer and the colonized is a colonial construct, i.e., he insists that neither the colonizer nor the colonized could exist without colonialism. Colonialism produces both the colonizer and the colonized.

Memmi attempts to address the criticism that he is presenting a portrait of colonization strictly in economic terms by the following statements:

> I have been criticized for not having constructed my portraits entirely around economic structure, but I feel I have repeated often enough that the idea of that privilege is at the heart of the colonial relationship—and that privilege is undoubtedly economic. Let me take this opportunity to reaffirm my position: for me, the economic aspect of colonialism is fundamental. This book itself opens with a denunciation of the so-called moral and cultural mission of colonization and shows that the profit

motive in it is basic. I have often noted
that the deprivations of the colonized are
the most direct result of the colonized are
the almost direct result of the advantages
secured to the colonizer. However,
colonial privilege is not solely economic.
(47)

He wants to extend his analysis of colonialism
to include the destruction of the social and
cultural institutions of the colonized, pointing
out the daily humiliation and subjugation
suffered by colonized people. Memmi sets out
to contrast psychoanalysis and Marxism with
the hope of discovering the sources of human
behavior. The goal is to analyze human
interaction and relationships within the context
of colonialism.

Insofar as what he initiates in his project,
Memmi causes us to question how we are to
determine what principles dictate human
relationships. Can we suggest that human
behavior is characterized by more than
economic relations? How can Memmi escape
Marx's conclusions? How does Memmi escape
colonialism? These are some of the questions
that arise in terms of the successful liberation

of the oppressed. The answers plot their successful escape from oppression. Therefore, it is by analyzing the other dimensions of eniyan reality that provides us with the solution. A simple presentation of the situation of the oppressed does not allow them to escape the process of colonization and the dependency on the colonizers for conceptualizations. In attempting to be very careful, I do not wish to attack the integrity of AfRaKan thinkers who have been Marxists because they represent genuine attempts to deal with human problems. Neither are we to attack Marx's integrity as well. What we do attack because our lives depend on it, is the Asiatic-centrism that appears in Marxism and AfRaKan thinkers. AfRaKan thinkers have especially brought to our attention the complexities of being oppressed and have provided us with very useful information. I am only suggesting that the destruction of the barriers in which Asiaticentrism has entrapped its victims has to be taken to higher levels. For the most part, the impact of Eurocentrism (colonialism, capitalism, Marxism, racism, e.t.c...) on the oppressed and their societies has been explicated in terms of its disruption of the indigenous economic institutions, and therefore, the interruption of the social and political institutions. Colonization has been classified in terms of privileges and disadvantages within its structure. The point is, what about its disruption of the cycle of life established by the colonized generations and generations before colonialism? What about the age-old wisdom before attempts at industrialization? Memmi says that:

He suggests here that colonialism creates barriers that separate the colonizer from the colonized. The colonizer is any person who lives in a colony, but at the same time, his nationality or mother country connects him with the colonial force. However, distinctions can be made to the extent that the eniyan is willing to accept his status as a colonizer. But their mere presence makes them colonizers.

A colonizer who refuses to accept his position as a colonizer is called a colonial. In most cases, this person's moral convictions will not allow him to accept the benefits of exploitation and oppression derived from the subjugation of the colonized. This person's economic status is very similar to that of the colonized. It is the consequence of his ineffectiveness and loss of power that occurs when he recognizes the dreadfulness of colonialism. His best option is to depart from the colony because he is unable to disconnect himself from the colonizers that share her nationality, and she is unable to connect herself with the colonized. To disconnect herself from the colonizer is to do the same with the mother country. This is impossible because she cannot identify with the natives whose culture and civilization she judges and discards as primitive. The colonial has to admit that a fundamental difference separates her from the colonized. A difference that emerges from two radically opposed historical experiences. The colonial must recognize that her Caucasian heritage has shaped her personality and tastes. She can reject her identification with the brutal colonial masters, but she cannot reject her culture and preferences, her sympathies towards the mother country. She is unable to adapt to the mood and needs of the colonized.

The colonial, or colonizer who refuses to admit that she/he is a colonizer, exists in a state of dichotomy. He admits, indirectly, that he pretends he is frightened and embarrassed by acts of terrorism, the possibility of war, the Koran, and a possible Arab League. The nationalistic and ethnic form of liberation excludes the colonial Caucasian mentality, making him a useless being.

> The left-wing colonizer refuses to become part of his group of fellow citizens. At the same time, it is impossible for him to identify his future with that of the colonized. Politically who is he? Is he not an expression of himself, of a negligible force in the varied conflicts within colonialism. (49)

As soon as the colonized recognize the ineffectiveness of the left-wing colonizer, he becomes insignificant. Therefore, Memmi's analysis suggests a final confrontation between the colonizer and the colonized. The colonizer, the brute who accepts his ambiguous position and adjusts his ideology to justify his conduct, is the medium through which colonialism paints its deceptive portrait of the colonized.

The existence of the colonizer supports the impression made on the colonized by colonialism. All the myths, stereotypes, injustices are the colonizer's doings—all on behalf of the structures of colonialism.

The colonizer himself is a usurper, a person who displaces the colonized. His birthright grants him privileges and benefits, and the colonial structures ensures that his children will receive the same. Each benefit, however, is derived from the misfortunes of the colonized. The colonizer benefits from a relationship in which he writes the colonized out of history. He accomplishes this in his glorification of the mother country as the seat of goodness.

Over the years, he has sculptured in opposition to the colony such a moment of his homeland that the colony necessarily appears coarse and vulgar to the novitiate. As though their homeland was an essential component of the collective superego of the colonizers, its material features become quasi-ethical qualities. The mother country thus combines only positive values, good climate, harmonious landscape, social discipline, and exquisite liberty, beauty, morality, and logic.

The colonizer moves to make his reality even though it is based on the perpetuation of falsehoods, the reality that the colonized must accept. This would explain why he doesn't hesitate when he finds the colonized attempting to assimilate and duplicate his model. But the colonized enter into assimilation by rejecting their uniqueness, their historically produced selves. They become the myths and stereotypes painted by the colonizers, and they begin to recognize his methods and values as superior. They give in to the right of the colonizer to dictate their destinies. The colonizers are thus justified in shaping the worlds of the colonized. Memmi has referred to this process as assimilation.

What is important here is that the colonized feel that they can end the relationship that exists in the colonial context by becoming the construct of the colonizers. He hopes that the colonizer will shape him into being, i.e., he places his faith in the colonizer so to become equal. However, Memmi believes that assimilation and colonization are in opposition to each other. The nature of colonialism creates a dichotomy from which the colonized benefits from the perpetuation of distinctions. In other words, the colonized are said to be backward and in need of management, and the colonial structures provide that management. If there is no need for management and the structures disappear, the colonized will not be able to justify benefitting from the relationship. The end of the significant place on distinctions means as end to the colonizer's privileges. For Memmi the answer is a revolution that overturns the economic and political exploitation. He concludes that:

> The liquidation of colonization is nothing but a prelude to complete liberation, to self-recovery. In order to free himself from colonization, the colon1ized musts start with is oppression, the deficiencies of his group. In order that his liberation may be complete, he must free himself from those inevitable conditions of his struggle. (51)

Memmi should also have mentioned that the process of self-recovery also means escaping the colonial construct of the colonized. An important aspect of self-recovery is how the self views itself. Colonialism is like a disease that enters a body and distorts its equilibrium by attacking the genes. As an effect, it causes the discoloration of the skin. In order to treat it, one could attempt to cover the skin with make-up to appear healthy. However, underneath [internally], there is no equilibrium and no health. Once the makeup evaporates, the same feeble condition resurfaces. To make my point, colonialism has removed the colonized from their natural setting in space and time. In the process, it has placed them in a position of bad health. It has maladjusted the colonized with their own being and therefore alter the course of their existence. Without a direct attempt to recapture their equilibrium with self, which in essence is self-directedness, assimilation is necessary, unavoidable, catastrophic result. It is true that the oppressed suffer from a disadvantageous economic relationship which the colonialism causes through economic disfranchisement. However, it does not follow that even after the usurpation of the colonized by the colonizer, the relationship would be okay if there was no economic disfranchisement. Sorry to say, but this reflects the impact of Caucasian thinking on these intellectuals. For example, Marx was caught up in analyzing a society by its mode of production, i.e., its economic institutions. He never addressed colonialism because to address the problems caused by colonization in terms of its economic relationships alone does not completely address colonialism. To escape colonialism is to be able to escape even Marxist analysis. It must return the colonized to their pre-colonial historical being. It is here that the colonized will be able to understand his personality and assess the direction of his future. He analyzes colonialism, for example, in respect to how it conflicts with his perspective on reality. Otherwise, they will find themselves assimilating to the colonizer's ideology. Marx's materialism alters the direction of society from their precolonial world-views in the same sense that colonialism does.

That is because Asiatic-centrism cannot account for the existence of the realities outside of its own boundaries. Its prism has been shaped by its own historical experiences. It has almost no connection with the ancestral world and its influence on phenomenon. Hence, for the Caucasian scientist, the role of spiritual incantations has no relevance on social structures and is nothing more than nonsense. A materialist worldview is unacceptable for the serious thinker because it is grounded on the same principles that dictate the mentality of the colonizer who refuses. It is unable to adjust to the possibility that the colonized is shaped by forces of a spiritual or ancestral world. Thus, colonialism affects all realities of the non-static colonized.

On these grounds, concentrating simply on an economic analysis does not allow us to escape from colonialism. It does not bring forth the possibility of decolonization from the structures of colonialism. The essence of the colonized cannot be captured in terms of privileges and economic relationships. The colonized cannot liberate themselves by ending the unequal relationships alone, and an approach towards decolonization is not found in the colonial relationships. It is found by momentarily escaping them through the resurrection of tradition.(52)

Section 1

WHERE LIBERATION TAKES US

Liberation takes us to the place where self-recovery begins. Self-recovery is the process by which we fully understand our orientation to the world in terms of positioning. Capturing the essentials in the positions of various AfRaKan intellectuals allows us to trace and piece together what has become AfRacentricity in its finality. Walter Rodney's concept of "underdevelopment" illustrates the importance of positioning in analysis. Clearly, Rodney is fully conscious in his works of the need for an AfRaKan perspective on colonialism. Also, Rodney is not strictly confined to just the economic disparities that colonialism caused. He seems to be more genuinely concerned with the way colonialism interrupted Africa's natural pattern towards development.

> All countries named as "underdeveloped" in the world are exploited by others, and the underdevelopment with which the world now is preoccupied is a product of capitalist, imperialist, and colonialist exploitation. AfRaKan and Asian societies were developing independently until they were taken over directly or indirectly by the capitalist powers.(53)

Rodney's analysis motivates us to review the possible impact that loss of population had on AfRaKan society. Ghana went from being one of the most richest cultural centers in the world to a place depleted of its majesty in matter of a few years. The impact of the slave trade on Africa was that it took all the artisans and craftsmen, leaving the weak behind. It also completely destroyed AfRaKan forms of royalty and anything that resembled AfRaKan forms of social organization.

What makes Rodney's critique more appropriate as a pillar in an AfRaKan centered method is that he recognizes Europe's amnesia when it comes to colonialism.(54)   Rodney, like W.E.B. Dubois, believed that the slave trade made the accumulation of wealth that Europe had acquired possible.

> The most spectacular feature in Europe which was connected with AfRaKan trade, was the rise of seaport towns--notably Bristol, Liverpool, Nantes, Bordeaux, and Seville. Directly or indirectly connected to those ports, there often emerged the manufacturing centers, which gave rise to the Industrial Revolution. In England, it was the county of Lancashire, which was the first center of the Industrial Revolution, and the economic advance in Lancashire depended

first of all on the growth of the port of
Liverpool through slave trading. (55)

Slavery as the economic foundation of the
Industrial Revolution is missing in Marxism. The
redistribution of wealth on an equalitarian basis
covers up that fact that the way that the wealth was
derived has had a tremendous impact on African
humanity. In Other Words, by destroying Africa,
Europe accumulated material wealth through the
monopolization of the world's resources. Before
AfRaKans address the issue of economic
readjustment and the possibility of reparations, an
analysis of the impact of colonialism on the
destruction of their humanity takes priority.

Section 2

METHODOLOGY AND PAN AFRAKAN CRITIQUE:THE PREOCCUPATION WITH AFRAKANITY

When the term "AfRaKan" becomes the focal point of a particular question, e.g., "Is there an AfRaKan World," or "Is there an AfRaKan Philosophy',' or any other AfRaKan "this or that," the response is asserted in a negative and/or often pejorative manner. It is assumed by skeptical inquisitors that there is no such thing as "Africa". Furthermore, they conclude that the rejection of an AfRaKan "something" is justifiably based on an inference from a "Caucasian" creation and/or misrepresentation of what we call Africa or AfRaKan. In other words, "Europe" created these notions of a unified concept of Africa and imposed it on the geographical Africa for economic and political purposes. Thus, (as it is argued by "Caucasian" and some "AfRaKan" scholars), the concept of "Africa" itself is a mythological construct, reflective of the fruit of "Caucasian' and Islamic" colonialism in what is referred to as "Africa". Armed with this radioactive assertion, some scholars have included in their dialectics the fabrication of an inter-African colonialism, i.e., an Ethiopian, Zulu, and Yoruba "ethnic" imperialism existing between AfRaKan people and having its origins in the colonial scramble for AfRaKan territories.

In reaction to domination, various AfRaKan ethnic groups wanted to take advantage of the exploits of colonialism. Therefore we are warned to be suspicious of an "invented" Ethiopia because these inventions reflect AfRaKan colonialism implemented by one ethnic group over another. Immediately in questioning the existence of an AfRaKan philosophy, we also discover an implicit attack on the idea of an Africa and AfRaKan humanity. Consequently, in order to avoid such misleading references to Africa, it is necessary to provide an AfRaKan- produced concept of Africa. Mudimbe justifies the assertion of an invented Africa by relating it to the Caucasian archaeology of knowledge. (56)

The attempt by Caucasian anthropologists to produce a hierarchy of human civilization resulted in the fabrication of Africa as a primitive division of humanity.

> In fact, from a more general historical frame, one can observe three complementary genres of_speeches contributing to the invention of a primitive Africa: the exotic text on savages, represented. by travelers'

reports, the philosophical interpretations about a hierarchy of civilizations, and the anthropological search for primitiveness. (57)

Although it is understandable why Mudimbe is skeptical of a Caucasian invented AfRaKa, it is not universally accepted that all concepts of a unified AfRaKa have been influenced by foreign domination. What about an AfRaKa produced for and by AfRaKans? Have AfRaKans always been the receptors of foreign meanings and not the creators of their own? The debate over this issue brings us to a confrontation between AfRacentricity, AfRaKan Studies, and Philosophy. (58)

In the works of AfRaKan scholars (Paulin Hountondji, Peter Bodunrin, and others), we discover subtle references to character defects that enable us to reflect and develop independent solutions to our problems. This explains why AfRaKan Philosophy is divided into various classifications: Professional Philosophy; Ethnophilosophy; cultural Philosophy; Political Philosophy; and finally, Philosophic Sagacity. It is important to understand who applies these distinctions and why? The movement of Afrocenrism confronts the concept that AfRaKans are dumbfounded receivers of ideas as opposed to the creators of their own meanings. AfRaKan intellectuals must walk the precarious path that steers away from these Euro typical claims about AfRaKans. We must assert a non-static methodology to defend ourselves and progress concerning traditional realities, even though what usually gets the label traditional also receives stigmatization as if it is no longer needed. Some can be relieved argue that tradition from duty by modernization through industrialization. In doing so, the problems associated with the Western approaches to development are overlooked because the benefits supposedly outweigh the imperfections.

The double standard is that the inability to accept AfRaKan imperfections is what leads to the consideration of the imperfections that the West has to offer. Still, the Caucasian imperfections are preferable regardless of the validity of this claim; the suggestion is that AfRaKans have a defect. Capitalism, Marxism, modernization become the tools to promote a nonindigenous model for development as well as medicine for AfRaKan backwardness. However, this is precisely a reflection of the imperialist premise. Europe came to Africa in order to civilize the "savages". Therefore what is imposed is the measure "Let Europe lead to us towards enlightenment". Although contemporary AfRaKan intellectuals would have us to believe that they are refuting the imperialist foundations of Western thinking, the argument that AfRaKan traditions are to be sacrificed for modernization reinforces the notion that Europe is the model of enlightenment. When we internalize our own supposed inferiority, no one has to "whip" us anymore because now we begin "whipping" our own selves.

Bodunrin and Hountondji have articulated the following positions, respectively:

> Philosophy in Africa has for more than a decade now been dominated by the discussion of one compound question, namely, is there an African philosophy, and if there is what it is? The first part of the question has generally been unhesitatingly answered in the second part of the question as various specimens

of African philosophy presented do not seem to pass muster. (59)

> I try to understand why most AfRaKan authors, when trying to engage with philosophy, have so far thought it necessary to project the misunderstood reality of their own discourse onto such palpable fiction. (60)

In offering what can be considered as metaconditions for the possibility of an AfRaKan Philosophy, both authors also suggest how it should be measured. Hountondji thinks we should be "scientific" because "science" is universal. Some have concluded that science and/or scientific theory is not value-laden. Unless we can determine its relevance, the imposition and acceptance of a blanket reference by Hountondji does not underrate our methodology. However, our methodology must have the sensitivity to appropriate these types of refutations while at the same time developing in different directions. The "New School" of AfRaKan intellectuals must pinpoint the impact of Caucasian studies on AfRaKan studies as well as absorb critically the works of "Old School" AfRaKan intellectuals.

Research into AfRaKan history has provided the refutation for some of the claims made about Africa in ignorance. We no longer have to accept Bodunrin's conclusions about philosophical problems:

> The thoughts of the ancient Greeks belong to the history of Western Philosophy, but the ancient Greeks and ancient Britons were mutually ignorant of each other.(61) And No one laments our late start in mathematics.(62)

Considering that AfRaKan scholars have contested the basis of these claims and offered us an alternative interpretation of history, the advent of an AfRacentric idea, although it is now resurfacing and becoming apparent in its embryonic stage, can surely serve to liberate the AfRaKan studies. AfRacentricity is changing the way we conceptualize reality. Its recovery appears to be an insistent yet gradual process. Here we discover the importance of the work of the Diopian scholars as a continuing process in an AfRaKan movement towards liberation. Their work has provided us with the basis for a truly AfRacentric critique of reality first, and then Asiatic-centrism and colonialism. How timely is the emergence of AfRacentrism in terms of AfRaKan consciousness? But, some of the most adamant critics of an AfRacentric idea have maintained the impossibility of referring to a distinctly AfRaKan "something". In My Father's House by Anthony Appiah represents a classical account of this attack. Appiah, with some intellectual vigor, argues that because of the degree of hybridization between various "cultures" and "races", it is impossible to refer to distinct human groups and independently developing societies. The problem reflects power relations, though, because Africa is not in a position to refute an attack of this nature. It is immediately understood when we compare it to the fact that these same intellectuals are not attacking the notion of Caucasian "something". Therefore, instead of addressing the latter, they pass it off under the model as the natural course of human development.

To their credit, Dubois, and Nkrumah, although deeply grounded in a Marxist metaphysics, confronted the destruction of AfRaKan "somethingness". Dubois, e.g., concluded that race was only one of many features that offered a unifying concept for Pan AfRaKanism.

AfRaKan people, he said, share a history of common experiences, common beliefs, common needs, as well as a common enemy.

Nkrumah and Cabral understood that in order for Socialism to work in Africa, it would have to be AfRaKanized. What we are saying is that it is necessary to discover why other factors in Pan AfRaKan ideologies are not considered by modern AfRaKan thinkers, especially in terms of the analysis of AfRacentrism. AfRaKan thinkers have been bombarded with Caucasian sources for the analysis of their situations. Even so, they are attempting to reestablish AfRaKans as conscious participants in Human history and are not purposely trying to destroy an intrinsic concept of "Africa". As a matter of fact, for both Dubois and Nkrumah, the concept of one Africa is necessarily the focal point of the call for Pan AfRaKan unity. Yet, both are still critical of the devastating potential of the Caucasian version of Africa. Consider this example from Dubois:

> The singular thing about this Caucasian movement of aggression and dominance rationalization for it. Missionary effort during the nineteenth and early twentieth

century was widespread. Millions of pounds and dollars went into the "conversion of the heathen" to Christianity and the education of the natives. Some few efforts, as in Liberia and Sierra Leone, were made early in the nineteenth century to establish independent Negro countries, but this was before it was realized that political domination was necessary to full exploitation. (63)

Section 3

CAUCASIAN HEGEMONY IN AFRAKAN AMERICAN THOUGHT

Since our analysis is concerned with method, we want to explain what is genuine in the arena of Pan-AfRaKan Philosophy. At the same time, we should also concentrate on bridging the gaps in Pan-AfRaKan philosophy. Our investigation leads us to the current trends in AfRaKan American philosophy. Like AfRaKan Philosophy, it is also divided into various camps. There are: The Black Hermenueticists and Critical theorists; Black Marxist; Pan-AfRaKanist and Nationalist. As strange as it may appear, there is much common ground between what the Black Hemenueticists are doing and what the AfRaKan professional philosophers have engaged. Historical experience has also grounded most of the philosophical concerns of AfRaKans in America. This is mainly because they have existed in a society that promoted systematic oppression and exploitation of its peoples and disfranchised its African community. In the process, AfRaKans who became AfRakan American's geographical disconnection and socialization were denied public display of their cultural rights of passage and introduced to self-hatred. They were also suppressed like other human groups in America under the umbrella notion of a shared tradition which all human groups were supposed to constitute. The concept of America, being the product of Caucasian colonialist expansion, also inherited the universalist interpretation of reality which was a direct result of Caucasian capitalism and imperialism. As we mentioned previously, Europe attempted to identify itself with the Ancient Greeks and the major themes of Greek society. Thus the context of this shared tradition had already been dictated by Europe, and the rest of the world was encouraged by force to assume their appropriate positions

AfRaKan American thinkers also began to question the notions of Caucasian supremacy and the Caucasian hegemony. What they discovered was that even the so-called "liberal" American intellectuals, maligned with racist ideology, did not provide much insight outside of prescribing hope as a cure to America's unseen ability to change. The current debate in AfRaKan American thought entertains some very serious questions to the understanding of social philosophy. But colonialism is also a factor in AfRaKan American thought, and it has not been isolated to the continent.

Thus, the problem with modern AfRaKan American intellectualism is the refusal to bridge the gap in the methodology to consider AfRaKan sources as the foundation of an African American centering. In other words, AfRaKan American intellectuals have the incumbent task of picking up the mantle where Dubois and Garvey left out. This effort should also correspond with the effort of continental AfRaKans working in philosophy and cultural sciences. AfRaKan and AfRaKan American social thought needs a complete overhaul.

Similarly, the Black Hermeneuticists call for a critique of Africa/American social thought. They argue that one of the goals of the AfRaKan intellectual is to focus on his people's revival, their life after the death of America. In the case of Lucius Outlaw, the AfRaKan intellectual has the complicated task of awakening "the stones" as he refers to "the dispossessed and oppressed of the American social order", specifically AfRaKan people.

It appears more adequately stated by Vincent Harding, who grounded our obligation to the AfRaKan masses as our ability to

> speak the truth to our people, to speak the truth about our enemies all in order to free the mind, so that black men, women, and children may build beyond the banal, dangerous chaos of the American spirit, towards a new time.(64)

Their position is that the content and focus of AfRaKan American thought must be grounded in critical revolutionary praxis to provide clarity concerning our own life-world (being as a people historically, culturally, socio-politically, economically, and futuristically, in order to provide a viable means of existence for ourselves. True democracy cannot be realized for all Americans if this is not the case.

AfRaKan people must become transparent to these AfRaKan thinkers/philosophers. For it is in them that our calling, our thrust for liberation, is represented to the world. Their vocation is to represent our life-world as best as possible.

Outlaw suggests that we are responsible for reshaping American social structure, but first, we have to develop a common understanding of our own historically conditioned interests along with the interests of others. He suggests that AfRaKan/Americans participate actively within the Hermeneutic circle. The task of the AfRaKan intellectual leads him into conflict and battles with ideologies and oppressor groups. The intellectual must resist a naive rush to uncritical intellectual integration and refrain from making commitments to unfair relationships with other ethnic groups especially Caucasian ones. These traditions have been plagued by doctrines of racial superiority and false notions of universality, which in turn has led to narrowness and degenerated into scientism by concentrating on method.

Any movement toward integration without clarification would:

> Prove to be our undoing in addition to reinforcing our selfdenial, we would fail to be aware of historical tendencies and possibilities that are might struggle with others to realize and, in so doing,

condition a line of historical development that could lead to enhanced conditions of life for all and, in particular for the 'marginal' peoples in the present order of life.(65)

To summarize the argument to this point, Hermenueticists argue that thinkers have been committed to Caucasian apprenticeship and have perpetuated their own presumed inferiority in the process, while other groups have been successful in having their interests expressed through nationalism. They also argue that America has always been a nation of nations and that power resides in ethnic/ national groupings (via the social reflection of a power circling). It is the function of Black thinkers to judge America for what it is. Therefore, they must "break the psychological umbilical ties to intellectual paternalism". AfRaKaN thinkers must begin to stand on their own and commit themselves to improving the lives of AfRaKans and the oppressed of American social order. For this purpose, we must be willing to commit class suicide and "resort to the desert" in search of wisdom if necessary.

Our commitment will inevitably lead us to an encounter with a philosophy that helps us to:

> share in the refinement and perpetuation of critical intelligence as a practice of life that has as its goal raising to consciousness of historical practices, and blocked alternatives wh1ch if freed, might lead to life experienced as qualitatively-progressively different. (66)

Hermeneutical understanding is grounded in historically conditioned concerns. It is a process that grants the reclamation and interpretation of our life-world. The life-world consists of the life-praxes, i.e., the forms for expression that allow us to relate meaning and the understanding of our own being. Philosophy, in the interests of AfRaKan-Americans, is increased self transparency through a critical understanding of our life world. It becomes necessary to produce an "authentic hermeneutic" as one that engages in a dialogical encounter between interpreter and work that allows the interpreter to "hear the question" of the work. It is by sharing an appropriation of meaning that a common horizon between work and interpreter is created. The horizon represents the mediation between the interpreter and the partner/object. It allows the AfRaKan to reflect and reclaim her/his tradition by expressing historically grounded needs and concerns. Its description of our being must help us to

> achieve cultural integrity: i.e., to embrace where available, to construct were unavailable, those productions and expression of meaning that serve to reflect the self-affirmations of black people,' e.t.c....(67)

The suggestion supported by Outlaw that America is a nation of many nations through 1ts separateness of ethnic groups also implies that America is of many traditions. He doesn't commit himself to saying there has been a shared tradition, heritage, or culture among the various ethnic groups here. At the same time, he attributes the success of other groups (non-AfRaKan) with their ability to fuse their tradition with the foundation of American society either by nature or by choice or by both and thus reap the benefits from the socio-political-economical order.

Our dismay has resulted from an uncritical commitment to impractical ideologies and erroneous allegiances to the intellectual apprenticeships of our masters or oppressors. In other words, AfRaKans have misjudged American society and our overall global situation.

Through a commitment to the restoration and refinement of human existence, Outlaw believes that hermeneutic understanding in the interests of AfRaKans, and all other ethnic groups for that matter, is a mediation of traditions; a mutual agreement between traditions that will produce a common good or a more viable existence for a greater number of people. With a similar viewpoint, Cornel West suggests that the prophetic tradition of the AfRaKan American Protestant Church fused with the efficiency of a cultural theory. Social philosophy needs to be regenerated by throwing away the old and oppressive ideas of the past and opening the doors for new and more creative ideas. He also believes that the African American Church inherited the fiery outlawism of Martin Luther, for example, and combined it with a vocal religious

interpretation of the conditions of slavery.
Thus, for him:

> The AfRaKan appropriation of
> Christianity under the conditions of
> slavery in the USA, the land of freedom
> and_ opportunity in. the eye of many,
> produces a unique version of Christianity
> with strong prophetic tendencies. This
> Afro-American Christianity serves as the
> major resource upon which black people
> draw strength and sustenance in their
> encounter with the modern American
> capitalist order--as urban dwellers,
> industrial workers, bureaucratic
> employees, and franchised citizens. (68)

AfRaKaN Hermeneuticists can be commended
for recognizing the need to reinforce the
integrity of AfRaKan American tradition as
something that refutes the claims of racial
superiority by the current power structure. Both
west and Outlaw argue that in Europe's
assumption of its own racial superiority, its
method has led to deformations in the tradition
of Western philosophy. Thus, Caucasian
philosophy has concentrated on the method
because of its narrowness and degenerated into

scientism. The redeeming quality of an authentic hermeneutic is in the possibility of human liberation, and it represents the social function of philosophy. A hermeneutic is authentic when it produces a horizon that manifests a mediation in meaning between the interpreter and the observed work or object. Unfortunately, their critiques are not unique because they do not allow us to escape the confines of the structures being critiqued, which is the Caucasian hegemony in modern philosophical explorations.

In recognizing all the problems associated with thought, AfRaKan and AfRaKan American thinkers still Western remain committed to investigating and prioritizing Europe in their thought processes. Never have they been committed to a persistent analysis to other forms of thought. As a result, these thinkers have caused various misunderstandings.

Implicitly, they assert that culture, tradition, and world view are synonymous with each other, meaning that one cannot exist without the other. West qualifies what it means to belong to a group or be part of a tradition, with the notion of a shared "world view".

Outlaw generalizes the existence of "AfRaKans" and "Afro-Americans", by assuming we all share a common "world view". However, his interpretation of AfRaKan/American existence does not fill the gap. For example, history shows us that different AfRaKans in America have held different world views" and still expressed their AfRaKanity.

Nonetheless, most thinkers have equivocated the restoration and refinement of human interests of AfRaKans (in America)' consensus, the practical which connects (to a greater degree) a common people with a common culture and tradition, with the revolutionary transformation of American socio\political\economic order. In retrospect, they have aligned culture and tradition with a "world view" or life praxis unambiguously. This does not fare well with historical examples and presents several inconsistencies. A perfect example is the relevance of "Black Radicalism" to the historical development of AfRaKans in this country. For instance, David Walker, who published "Walker Appeals" in September of 1829, urged Black people to:

Let your Enemies go with their hatred and at once fill up their cup. Never make an attempt to gain our freedom or natural rights, from under our cruel oppressors and murderers, until you see your way clear-when that hour arrives and you move, be not afraid or dismayed; for be you assured that Jesus Christ the King of Heaven and earth who is the God of justice of armies, will surely go before you. And those enemies who have for hundreds of years stolen our rights, and kept_us ignorant of him (God) and his divine worship, he will remove.(69)

Walker identifies his enemies as:

The system of slavery and its advocates in the North and South alike the American government, which supported that system and other aspect of white supremacy; and the white citizens of the country of large who co-operated 1n any way in the degradation of Black People. (70)

If we accepted the generalized concept of tradition, a person like David Walker, who did not believe in "the revolutionary transformation of American social order" (which Outlaw calls worldview of AfRaKan Americans), and instead believed that AfRaKan Americans should look outside of America for solutions, would not be part of that tradition and therefore, not a person of AfRaKan descent. Furthermore, according to Outlaw, there is nothing that separates people from different cultures that share a common worldview. The AfRaKans and "Jews" who fought for civil rights would appear to be part of the same tradition. This is very problematic given the nature of AfRaKan American relations with other groups in this country. Therefore we assert that the concept and range of AfRaKan history is too limited and causes an inability to capture the full spectrum of AfRaKan experiences. Their "worldview" captures the best of maybe Frederick Douglas, Dr. Martin Luther King, and several others. But it leaves out the significance of Denmark Vessey, Gabriel Prosser, and the massive slave revolts in north and south America. It partially represents AfRaKan Heritage. West has the gap that Habermas recognizes is unavoidable if the interpretation and the canon disagree fundamentally. It is evident that a conceptual problem exists in outlaw philosophical base.

Section 4

SPIRITUALITY AND THE SOULS
OF BLACK FOLK

AfRaKan Americans have a particular type of spirituality that remains unexplainable by Western methods. When attempts are made to utilize these methods, AfRaKan Americans appear as incomplete beings. This occurs by overlooking the structure of AfRaKan American social contexts. In the majority of cases, especially with AfRaKan Americans from the South, spirituality determines social activity on all fronts. Extended family concepts are prevalent in Southern communities. Also, elders maintain centers of authority in most family and community activities. The whole idea of Black family reunions attempts to bring families together as well as an opportunity to show respect for the older (or seasoned as my Aunt often remarks} members of the family. AfRaKan Americans from all over the country will migrate to the South for these celebrations.

Philosophically, the task is to try and explain these types of occurrences. However, it is essential that an AfRaKan framework is employed to do so.

Mainly because:

> It was from within an African framework that the slaves made adjustments to Christianity after hearing the gospel. The influences of the African religious past extended into their new life, first in the Caribbean and later in the United States, and, far from being completely obliterated, were reshaped by the circumstances of enslavement.

Section 5

AFRACENTRISM, MOLEFI ASANTE , TRADITIONAL PHILOSOPHERS, AND OTHERS

Although the previous thinkers could have been in the right direction, the AfRaKan world awaits a more viable method. The injecting of an AfRacentric idea allows us to look at the aspects of AfRaKan existence by using an AfRaKa produced model of existence. If we further investigate AfRacentrism, we discover the possibility to uniquely reexamine the way of life of our collective past. Therefore, in discovering the retentions carried by the captives (the "chattel" slaves) to the Caucasian world and the many AfRaKan contributions to world culture which have not been acknowledged, AfRacentrism appears to initiate at the point where Pan AfRaKanist like Dubois concluded. Consequently, the prescription of a Pan AfRaKan analysis must continue to remain versatile enough to capture the needs of an all-AfRaKan method. Some thinkers have found it necessary to offer definitions to an "AfRacentric" idea and have tried to steer clear from the contamination usually associated with methods. For Molefi Asante, the challenge for the Afrocentrist is to:

> Maintain inquiry rooted in a strict
> interpretation of place in order to betray
> all naive racial theories and establish

AfRacentricity as a legitimate response to the human condition. All knowledge results from an occasion of encounter in place. But the place remains a righty-shaped perspective that allows the Afrocentrist to put AfRaKan ideals and values at the center of inquiry. (73)

An exploration to be Africa-logical must be based on sound intellectual and Philosophically of the foundations which maintain the centrality of the AfRaKan experience and the primacy of classical traditions. (74)

The structure of Afrocentric inquiry is shaped to a large extent by what can be categorized by five principal issues. These are aesthetic axiological, cosmological, and epistemological questions. The questions reflect, through AfRaKan concepts, the dynamic AfRaKa position in the cosmos, i.e., ideals index. The basis or that shapes the AfRaKan "cosmo-cultural" index. The basis of the foundation is provided by the AfRaKan origins of civilization. (75) Kemetic high culture and civilization serve as the fundamental principle which allows the scholar to evaluate its impact on Africa and AfRaKan phenomena. From this perspective, one can identify central themes that permeate AfRaKan societies. At the same time, one recognizes the AfRaKan contribution to world civilization and culture.

Also, AfRaKan behavior on levels becomes comprehensible. Diop has argued that the historical significance of Egypt represents developments within the AfRaKan attempts at civilization as well as spiritual and intellectual achievements. Africa and Egypt are seen as interconnected and interrelated occurrences. AfRaKan languages retain symbols, words, and concepts that also appeared in Pharaonic Egyptian tongue. The psychological impact of sharing a common history of interrelatedness is evident in religious and cultural institutions as well as other social institutions. In other words, shared perceptions and shared understandings for meaning offer a unifying metaphysical orientation to reality that is uniquely holistic in most cases. One essential problem that deserves immediate clarification is how this does not mean that all AfRaKans share the same exact values, but it does assert that they have more in common than they do that differs. The commonalities present us with what can be called retentive cultural identities. These identities formulate a sort of cultural nationalism existing in pre colonial Africa. Thus AfRaKans are not shaped into being by foreigners but have pre-existing institutions responsible for their socialization. The post-Christian interpretation of Africa puts her on the run from various colonizers and limits itself to the fruit of their invasions. It created a sense of cultural and historical amnesia in the world in terms of rejecting distinctly AfRaKan contributions.

Section 6

AFRACACENTRISM AND THE RECOVERY OF TRADITIONAL AFRICA

The most progressive works in the arena of Pan AfRaKan thought seem to be in the works of the AfRacentrists and those who call themselves Cultural Philosophers. Whereas the AfRacentrists are trying to reconstruct a legitimate interpretation of AfRaKan traditions, the Culturalists are investigating the relationship between traditional AfRaKan thought and the contemporary AfRaKan world. Thus, the AfRacentrist and the Cultural Philosopher mutually correspond with each other. The usual disagreement, in this case, is that both groups tend to overgeneralize AfRaKaN customs. It is argued that what is true in a particular AfRaKan setting might not be true in another. Nevertheless, the confusion over this matter relates to the central Diopian point that Lancinay Keita captures eloquently:

> The above discussion on the African philosophical tradition constitutes an attempt to present a framework in which discussion on the major thought systems of Africa could take place. Consistent with the methodology of the formulation of the dominant thought systems of a whole people, no attempt was made to incorporate into the AfRaKan

philosophical framework the folkways of thinking of Africa's diverse people. Such an approach leads to confusion and the paralyzing of any attempts at creating a genuine structure of AfRaKan Thought. The ways of thinking of Africa's diverse peoples are significant from the philosopher's point of view only in the sense that they resemble classical AfRaKan thought in embryonic form. (76)

There are also others like Kwame Gyekye, Wale Soyinka, Segun Gbadegesin, e.t.c., who are using traditional belief systems to develop an AfRacentric approach to Philosophy. Akan and Yoruba belief systems are explicated in terms of how AfRaKans perceived the world. Therefore, they offer us a tool for determining whether an AfRacentric method works in a Pan AfRaKan context. The possibility that the Culturalists are AfRacentrists is finally very important. In a true sense, the determining characteristic AfRaKan philosophy is the incorporation of an AfRacentric method. No human endeavor is unstained by a particular cultural/social heritage.

An AfRacentric philosopher assumes that she/ he is working under these conditions upon beginning. Objectivity, then, has no content outside of the subjective values placed within it. It is not the primary goal of the Afrocentrist to be "objective".

In America, we find the example of the Gullah people, who have maintained an AfRaKan (AfRacentric) way of life. The key is AfRaKans have been and would be AfRacentric even if there were no threats.. Thus Europe has promoted an ethnocentric universalism that the world must escape. The guest for Afrocentrists as well as all others concerned about their cultural heritage, is to divorce themselves from this circle and return to the groundings of their ancestors: to return to true self-formative activities and to stop chasing after Europe. It may sound radical, but in essence, it is to promote peace within this world. Diop argued that what is central to understanding AfRaKan civilization and thought are these key facts:

1. The anteriority of Africa as the birthplace of Humanity and Civilization.

2. The AfRaKanity of the Classical AfRaKan civilizations such as Kemet (Egypt) and Nubia.

3. The impact of classical Africa on language and thought systems on other AfRaKan civilizations.

4. The impact of Africa on the knowledge systems on world civilizations (which would include Asian, Greek, and Caucasian attempts at civilization)

5. The philosophical and scientific impact of Africa on World knowledge.

6. The need for an AfRacentric interpretation of reality in modern developments and the liberation of the AfRaKan mind based on this interpretation.

In providing us with their analysis, the cultural philosophers reinforcing Diop's main objective: African somethingness. The implication solves the question that demarcates the various regimes in AfRaKan philosophy. (77) Although it remains important to understand the types of questions that one proceeds to ask in a discussion on tradition or Immanuel Kant, what is primary is that they remain AfRaKan centered in doing so. An AfRaKan-centered philosopher finds relevance in a literate or non-literate tradition. The method required must be diverse enough to allow for it. Though writing is important, it is not the final and determining factor as far as a philosophical centering is concerned. A classic example is how Presocratic Greeks were, in most cases, non-writers, but later with Plato, writing becomes essential to philosophy. In both cases, the relevance of writing to understanding the movement of Greek thought has only become prioritized because writing has always been a part of the meta-conditions of philosophy. Nevertheless, no one has doubted the impact of Thales and Pythagoras to Greek thought. AfRaKan philosophy does not need to hold itself liable to a criterion that demands writing.

However, it must remain within the context of the movement of the AfRaKan world. Gbadegesin seems to agree on this issue:

> My own view is that AfRaKan philosophy is first and foremost a philosophical activity and is addressed to issues relating to AfRaKan realities - traditional or contemporary. By the later, I mean that is satisfies any or all of the following:
>
> It focuses on African conceptual systems, (ii) It deals with problems and issues AfRaKan in Nature, (iii) it is based on contemporary African Experience (iv) it is a comparative study and analysis of African realities vis-à-vis other regions of the world. (76)

SUMMARY

Due to the brainwashing engines encoded in American culture's very fabric, AfRaKan American scholarship has been critical of such trends and has provided crucial intellectual support towards the recovery and restoration of an AfRaKan worldview. This would also include AfRaKan Caribbean scholars and leaders whose significance has been underrated. As is the case, the ascendancy of an AfRacentric idea has been built on a variety of disciplines as opposed to a concentration in the area of "Philosophy" proper. Historians like Carter G. Woodson maintained that AfRaKan people should have an innate self-produced understanding. The form of self-understanding would allow them the consciousness to liberate themselves from the constraints of Western oppression. Bringing down the Berlin Walls of Western oppression will allow AfRaKan intellectuals to produce a progressive literature calling for the liberation of AfRaKan people. In reference to the AfRacentric approach, Molefi Kete Asante has said:

> The AfRacentric enterprise is framed by cosmological, epistemological,

axiological, and aesthetic values. In this regard, the AfRacentric method pursues a world voice that's distinctly AfRaKan-centered in relationship to external phenomena... Although I recognize the transitional nature of all cultural manifestations of a social, economic, or political dimension, I also know the African world, culturally speaking, there is a movement toward new, more cosmo-cultural forms of understanding. (79)

We must insure that we carry out our analysis in relation to AfRaKan cultures and values, continental and worldly. Therefore, it is necessary to connect the need for what AfRaKan Americans say about their AfRaKan culture and values with what the culturalist say about their AfRaKan culture and values. The product of such a connection surfaces as a Pan AfRaKan discussion about AfRaKan world views. The method employed must embrace a revitalization in the way AfRaKans visualize themselves, thus producing an autonomous interpretation. If it does not occur, we will find ourselves guilty of uncritical intellectual integration appealing to foreign methodologies as tools to help us in self-understanding.

Nevertheless, AfRacentrism should attempt to avoid the deformations of the philosophy practiced in the West.

The AfRaKan person, both as questioner and observer, becomes an AfRaKan looking inward: What was my own doing in the situation that brought me here today? What are my historical failures and achievements? The AfRaKan employs tools that his forefathers developed. Perspectives emanating from a centering or prism give AfRaKans a vehicle to assert the nature of our relationship with the universe and the same time, escape the confines of Asiatic-centrism. Hence as is previously noted, our battle is not with Asiatic-centrism on a higher level, but only to the extent that we find ourselves subjugated by it. Also, the arguments for a sincere multicultural perspective do not conflict with an AfRacentric orientation. However, caution is employed since we have not divorced ourselves from the forces that enslave us. By nature, an AfRacentric idea is humanistic and has the flexibility to cooperate with other cultural perspectives. Given that the Asiatic-centrism has armored Asiatics with a false sense of place in human activity, it has also disconnected

Asiatics from humanity in a n attempt to keep non-Asiatics subjugated, which means it cannot be argued that Asiatic-centrism is flexible in terms of other cultures. It justifies why the subjugated cultural perspectives have to engage in battles to free themselves from Asiatic-centrism. In other words, Human consciousness has to be raised to a higher level where it will conquer the death caused by Asiatic-centrism. To be able to accomplish this goal, other perspectives will have to take precautionary measures, which include avoiding a rush to "universalism" and "objective" truths. Human consciousness must reveal itself as the result of various human centerings with various human truths. Malauna Karenga's Kawaida theory is such an attempt. With its Nguzo Saba, it centers values in an AfRaKan frame of reference.(80) By doing so, it has escaped the confines of intellectual dependency on other Perspectives and proceeded in the direction of considering its own as a valuable resource. So what we would call AfRacentric is constantly shaped by the movement of the centering as it encounters experiences.

It sees itself as posited in a cyclical relationship in reference to time and as a symbolic relationship between spirituality and materiality. Therefore, it becomes important to reinvestigate what gets passed as religion and what passes as science.

After all, science employs reason, whereas religion employs faith with a little reason and more emotion. But the idea of reason is very problematic because it is dialectical, existing in confrontation as opposed to harmony. The world of reason sees experience as a daily or lifelong war. The difference is that a symbolic understanding of reality produces a world that continuously searches for harmony. The AfRacentric perspective brings into question the fundamental basis for perspectives. Even though it may sound rhetorical, it is saying that human beings develop perspectives to protect their orientation to life and, therefore, their humanity.

CHAPTER IV: CONCLUSION: THE IMPLICATIONS Of AN AFRAKAN STUDIES REVOLUTION

The emphasis of this project is not to suggest that modern Cultural and AfRacentric Philosophers answered all of our questions. It is more so an attempt to utilize the discovery of generating an isolatable AfRaKan centered method that could revolutionize the approach to AfRaKan studies and then the AfRaKan world. The project is also seriously concerned with developing a way to actualize AfRacentricity with its goal: the complete liberation from a materialist preoccupation, destruction of the Caucasian hegemony in AfRaKan Studies, and a restoration of traditional world-views and practices as the foundation of AfRaKan and AfRaKan American investigation. AfRacentric thinkers and Cultural philosophers have opened the doors of inquiry to AfRaKan sources for alternative viewpoints in a world that moves further and further into the oblivion of Western decadence. Thereby, AfRaKan Studies should actualize the conclusions of these groups, and it can become a revolutionary activity in the interests of its Pan African community.

A primary step to an African-centered method in African Studies returning to the privatization of African sources presently, most African culture has been bombarded with Caucasian frames of reference in terms of language, methods, legitimators. AfRaKan thinkers must begin to communicate in indigenous languages with indigenous alphabets and symbols to solve this problem. Languages remain a powerful way of retaining and promoting culture. In this regard, there is a renewal driven by many to learn Medu Neter, driven by a desire to restore consciousness of a traditional AfRaKan world. To a greater degree, AfRaKa has kept its cultural institutions alive behind the scenes due to colonial attempts to acculturate her with Caucasian languages like Geez, Tigrinya, and Amharic, like the Abrahamic faiths, are instruments of Caucasian imperialism. As a result, the goal is to return to indigenous and traditional culture and refuse and reject all imported existential tools of control like Religion as economic doctrines like Capitalism, Socialism and Communism opting for communalism instead.

AfRaKans in America, like other AfRaKans, have been forced to hold on to various notable AfRaKan elements and AfRaKanized products from their new experiences. Colonialism attempted to replace what AfRaKan people had initially been with the existential identity of its colonizers. But the fact remains that AfRaKan in American English (or Ebonics) and African spiritual culture are in many forms of expression that have been flooded with Asiatics methods of control at the level of existence. AfRaKan in American culture, especially in the Southern parts of America, is a uniquely AfRaKan culture that should be seen as an African tentative cultural identity. The Abrahamic faiths were used to brainwash an identity crisis on the US population because it drives people to work thinking that they will be rewarded with a "heaven." When that didn't work, the trap that teaches to keep the work trap alive created a completely distorted identity, leading to masculine beings thinking that they give birth. This was forced on AfRaKan in America in particular. Still, many have retained and practiced AfRaKan culture due to advances in our scholarship, which is also reflected by the arakunrin Garfield Reid scholarship. This also proves that AfRaKan in Americans are not monolithic even though they share common experiences. AfRaKan America is as diverse as the AfRaKan continent itself. Blacks in the South are incredibly religious and practice extended family concepts. Hence, if

African Americans had a power base, it would have to come from the South since Too many Northern Blacks are too well dispersed and integrated into the Northern metropoles to effectuate profound change considering that many still live in the inner cities. Except for Detroit, or Chicago, there are more predominantly AfRaKan American cities in the South, and more blacks continue to migrate Southwardly daily in search of opportunities.

Thus, in establishing a Southern-based identity, combined with an AfRaKan based linguistic analysis of Ebonics and the usage of an AfRaKan Alphabet like Geez, the aggregation of AfRaKan American resources in this country, AfRaKan Americans could become the most influential ethnic group in their world. In understanding this power, they must also understand their responsibilities to Africa and its various calls for redemption.

It is not surprising then that the Civil Rights Movement was born in the South movement in the North Blacks. (82) However, even though the abolitionist in free states by the Northern ideological base of AfRaKan Americans produced these movements. I believe that both movements reflect a high degree of religiosity and a communal orientation inherent in the AfRaKan/African American experience transcendence of the foundation of a metaphysical framework instead of a materialist metaphysical framework.

The case being that integration thought, e.g., the desire for AfRaKan Americans to integrate into Caucasian America in the vague sense, but the desire to transcend the difference between two human groups. In comparison, Caucasian culture has not demonstrated the mentality necessary to produce a spiritual orientation to life. Feminists should analyze Classical music to understand the role of gender in musical arrangement and horn selection. However, in Jazz, you discover musical expressions in synthesis, polyrhythms, and AfRaKan religious orientations. (83)

In comparison, Caucasian culture has not demonstrated the mentality necessary to produce a spiritual orientation to life. Therefore, on an AfRaKan world scale, an African cultural revolution should consider replacing the Greek, Latin, and Arab languages with traditional or ancient AfRakan languages like the Medu Neter or a continental African language and alphabet restore a connection with the ancestors. Even in the case of AfRaKan American spiritual presence, we need to reject the Asiatic Existential Imperialism. This is where arakunrin Garfield Reid's research, as reflected in the book Misconceptions & Misinformation by the Black Hebrew Israelites Vol I, is a great asset and could serve as a liberating force. As beings, we need to reject the church entirely and focus our attention on science. This will allow us to rethink the Asiatic hegemony in our consciousness, including our notions of spirituality, which will enable us to decolonize ourselves.

Endnotes

1. There of human other is no reason that there cannot exist various models of human history that acknowledge mutual respect.

2. Eurocentrism, by Samir Amin, First edition, Monthly Review Press, 1989, pg.17

3. The Philosophers of Greece, by Robert Brambuagh,

4. It must be noted that Amin believes that characterized by communal modes of production are "primitive" and barbarous.

5. Black Athena, by Martin Bernal, Rutgers University Press, New Jersey, 1987,   pg. 1

6. Amin., pg. 4

7. Bernal, pg. 198

8. Amin., pg. 75

9. Amin., pg. 78

10. Aristotle explicitly associates morality with skin color and then moves to argue that the Greeks are inherently more "cultured" than others. See Aristotle's Nichomachean Ethics.

11. Stolen Legacy, by George James, United Brothers Communication Systems, Virginia, 1989

12. In Timaes, Plato says: "As I said at first when all things were in disorder God created 1n each thing in relation to itself, and in all things in relation to each other, all the measures and harmonies which they could possibly receive. For in those days, nothing had any proportion except by accident, nor did any of the things which now have names deserve to be named at all-as, for example, fire, water, and the rest of the elements. All these the creator first set in order, and out of them, he constructed the universe, which was a single animal comprehending in itself all other animals, mortal and immortal. Now of the divine, he himself was the creator, but the creation of the mortal he committed to his offspring. And they, imitating him, received from him the immortal principle of the souls". This is very similar to doctrines found in the "Book of the coming forth by day and night." When does the application of Egyptian ideas stop, and the Greek ones begin in Plato's writing?

13. see Herodutus• Histories, especially stanza 21

14. A New Aristotle Reader, edited by J.L. Ackrill, Princeton University Press, New Jersey, 1987, stanza 1107

15. ibid., stanza 1107

16. ibid.,

17. ibid., 1174

18. ibid., 1174

19. ibid., 442

20. Aristotle Reader, pg. 508, stanza 1252

21. see Temple in Man by Schwaller De Lubicz, Inner Traditions

International, Vermont, 1977

22. Ethnocentrism in History, by Preiwork and Perrot, New York:

Nok Publishers, 1974, pg. 34

23. Charles Taylor, Hegel, Cambridge University Press, New York,

1975 pg. 54

24. ibid., pg. 59

25. As we will discuss later in the section that Deals with Buddhist thought, where a similar proposition was suggesting that all things having a "buddha nature" is made.

26. ibid., pg. 77

27. In his critique of Immanuel Kant, Hegel rejects the notion of a "thing in itself."

28 The foreground of Hegel Dialectic; thesis, antithesis, and synthesis.

29. ibid., pg 89

30. ibid., 129

31. ibid., pg. 155

32. Robert C. Lester, Theravada Buddhism in Southeast Asia, University of

Michigan Press, Ann Arbor, 1973, pg. 26

33. William Theodore de Bary, The Buddhist Tradition in India, China, and Japan, Vintage Books, New York, 1969, pg. 143   .

34. A distinction is made between Western versions of Christianity and the Orthodox Egyptian version which has its roots in the AfRaKan practice of Osirianism. Like other African religious practices, it is customary not

to separate creation from the creator, the mind the body, and in this case Heaven from Earth. The fundamentals of Christianity being that they were not indigenous aspects of Western Society were altered to adjust to Western pagan forms of worship. Also, the emphasis on a strictly empirical and material interpretation of reality caused the need to place the universe into singular and separate categories. Furthermore, those things which were beyond the grasp of the Western mind were denounced as irrelevant and unrealistic. For further elaboration, the interested reader should consult the works of Yosef ben_Jochanan, Martin (Black Athena), and other non-European versions of the Bible.

35. E.A. Burtt, The teachings of the Compassionate Buddha, Mentor Books, New York, 1982, pg. 162

36. It is possible a reference to Buddhism here shows the ethnocentrism in Hegel's positions, the reason why Marx sought a new unity between theory and practice, and the possibility that Hegel was more influenced by the contemporary materialism of his time than most scholars have recognized.

37. The possibility of importing tools from foreign sources is tainted by the fact that the tools exist within a cultural context and are also value laden. It has not been determined as to how one can divorced foreign "tools". from there? Context and inject them into a new environment without damaging the prior cultural context.

38. Ujamaa: Essays on Socialism, Julius K, Nyrere, Second Edition, Oxford University press, London, 1970, pg. 109

39. Karl Marx and African Emancipatory thought: A critique of Marx's Eurocentric Metaphysics, by Tsenay Serequeberhan, Praxis International; 10:1/2, April & July 1990, pg. 162

40. ibid., pg. 161

41. ibid., pg. 163

42. Marx-Engels Reader, edited by Robert Tucker, Second edition, W.W. Norton & Company, New York, 1978, pg. 658

43. ibid., pg. 165

44. It has been falsely assumed that Marx was critiquing capitalized since he never critiqued

colonialism. Capitalism crystalized because of enhancement of colonialism by Europeans. Colonialism, therefore, should be reconsidered as both a force and relation of production in connection with Capitalism and Marxism. This is important because the next step would be to argue that since Marx was mainly analyzing the distribution of wealth, Socialism in not only inherently Eurocentric but also inextricably tied to colonialism. It is inherently tied to the evolution of European society as Marx sees it.

45. Civilization or Barbarism, by Cheikh Anta Diop, Presence Africaine, Paris 1981, pg. 317

46. ibid., pg. 205

47. Albert Memmi, The Colonizer and the Colonized, The Orion Press, Inc., U.S.A., 1965, p. xii

48. ibid., pg. 149-150

49. ibid., pg. 41

50. ibid., pg. 60

51.ibid., pg. 151-152

52. Nevertheless, meaning in the contemporary context must be derived from the most centered aspects of AfRaKan's being. When this is not

the case psychological dislocations creates automatons who are unable to fully capture the historical moment because they are living on someone else's terms. We are either existing on our own terms or the terms of others, where will the AfRaKan person find emotional and cultural satisfaction if not in her own terms? By term I mean position, place, or space (see Molefi Asante, Kemet, Afrocentrity, and Knowledge, pg. 8)

53. How Europe Underdeveloped Africa, by Walter Rodney, Bogle-L "Overture Publications, London, 1972, pg. 14

54. Rodney states that "even Marxist for many years concentrated on examining the evolution of capitalism out of feudalism inside Europe with only marginal reference to the massive exploitation of Africans, Asians, American Indians."

55. Rodney pg. 85

56. In The Invention of Africa, V. Y. Mudimbe asserts that the conception of a unified Africa is a European Construct.

57. The Invention of Africa, by V.Y. Mudimbe, First edition, Indiana University Press, Bloomington, 1988, pg.69

58. AfRacentricity is a theme that resonates throughout the existence of AfRaKans. It does not belong to a particular individual. However, their interaction with it has been significant to its development.

59. Peter Bodunrin, "The question of AfRaKan Philosophy" in African Philosophy, edited by Tsenay Serequeberhan, Paragon House, New York, 1991, pg. 6

60. ibid. "AfRaKan Philosophy: Myth and Reality," by Paulin Hountondji, pg. 112

61. ibid., pg. 8

62. ibid., pg. 8

63, The World and Africa, by W.E.B Dubois, International Publishers co., Inc., New York, 1965, pg. 33

64. Vincent Harding, "The Vocation of the Black Scholar and the Struggles of the Black Community." Harvard Educational Review, 1974, pg. 6

65. "Philosophy, Hermeneutics, Social-Political Theory: Critical Thought in the Interests of AfRaKan Americans," by Lucius Outlaw and edited by Leonard Harris in Philosophy born of Struggle, Kendall/Hunt Publishing Company, Iowa, 1983, pg. 61

66. ibid., pg. 65

67. ibid., pg. 71

68. Prophetic Fragments, by Cornel West, Wm B. Eerdmans

Publishing Co., 1988, pg. 67

69. There is a River, by Vincent Harding, pg. 87

70. ibid., pg. 34

71. Knowledge and Human Interests, by Jurgen Habermas, Beacon Press, Boston, 1968, pg. 165

72. Black Religion and Black Radicalism, by Gayraud S. Wilmore, second edition, Orbis Books, New York, 1986

73. Kemet, Afrocentricity, and Knowledge by Molefi Asante, First Edition, Africa World Press, New Jersey, 1990, pg. 5

74. ibid, pg. 56

75. As recent debate continues to offer testimony; Modern scholars continue to have a problem accepting the African origin of civilization.

76. And Keita continues with, "For a history of AfRaKan philosophy is coherent only in the sense that it recognizes as a definite stage in African thought the most literate moments of that particular era. The discussion focused on three distinct periods of Africa's s intellectual history. Its classical period was by far the most remarkable in that it was essentially of independent derivation and exercised important seminal influences on Hellenic and Medieval Europe and medieval Africa. See Lancinay Keita "The AfRaKan Philosophical tradition," in Richard Wright's AfRaKan Philosophy, University Press of America, Maryland, 1984, pg. 72

77. Professional, Ethnophilosophy, Political, and Cultural

78. AfRaKan Philosophy, by Segun Gbadegesin, Peter Lang, New York, 1990 pg. 22

79. Asante, pg. 8

80. Karenga, in many of his works, attempts, like Asante, to isolate an AfRaKan approach to understanding reality. See either Kemetic Worldview: Essays in Ancient Egyptian Studies, by Maulana Karenga and Jacob Carruthers, University of Sankore Press, Los Angeles, 1984 or Kawaida Theory, by Maulana Karenga, Kawaida Press, Los Angeles, 1980

81. See AfRaKanisms in American culture, edited by Joseph Holloway, Indiana University Press, Bloomington, 1991

82. Of course, this is not totally true because many abolitionists were former captives who escaped from the South to live in the "free" territories. The emphasis here to suggest that even Northern Blacks have remained closely knitted and responsible to the Southern Heritage.

83. Classical music, instruments are given gender roles and often portray male and female characters in the progression of a musical arrangement. Woodwinds are usually passive, and emotional instruments played passive and emotional instruments played by women

whereas. Brass, drums, and bass are domineering ones played by men. In Jazz, it is commonly known that the saxophone represents sex. But sex represents woman and man in unity as individuality is transcended. Also, in jazz arrangements, no particular horn or instrument has center stage. Instead, all work together to produce a good sound. Even solos are done with the participation of the other horns in the backdrop, or sometimes you can have simultaneous solos occurring.

Bibliography

Aldred, Cyril, Akhenaten: King of Egypt, by Thames and Hudson Inc., London 1988

Allen, E.L., From Plato to Nietzsche, Fawcett Premier Book, Great Britain, 1957

Amen, Ra un Nefer. Metu Neter, Khamit Corp., New York, 1990

Amin, Samir. Eurocentrism, Monthly Review Press, New York, 1989

Anmi, Ben. God, the Black Man and Truth Communication Press, Chicago, 1982   '

Appiah, Kwame Anthony. In My Father's House, Oxford University Press, New York, 1992 ·

Armah, Ayi Kwei. Two Thousand Seasons, Heinemann, Heinemann, London, 1987

Asante, Molefi Kete. The AfRacentric Idea, first edition, Philadelphia, Temple University Press, 1987

Asante, Molefi Kete. Kemet, AfRacentricity, and Knowledge, Africa World Press, New Jersey,   1990

Asante, Molefi. Thunder and Silence, Africa World Press, Inc., New Jersey, 1992

Baldwin, James. The Fire Next Time, Dell Publishing Co., New York, 1963

Bernal,   Martin. Black Athena II, first edition, U.S.A., Rutgers University Press, 1991

,

Bernal,   Martin. Black Athena, Rutgers University Press, New Jersey, 1989

Blavatsky, H.P., Isis Unveiled, vol I and II, Theosophical University Press, New York, 1877

Blavatsky, H.P., The Secret Doctrine, vol I and II, Theosophical University Press, London, 1888

Bond, George. AfRaKan Christianity, Academic Press, New York 1979

Burger, Luckmann. The Social Construction of Reality, Anchor Books, New York, 1966

Cabral, Amilcar. Revolution in Guinea, trans. by Richard Handyside, Monthly Reveiw Press, New York, 1968

Caldwell, Bruce. Beyond Positivism, George Allen Unwin Pub., London, 1983

Carson, Lionel. Ancient Egypt, Time Life Books, New York, 1965

Chan, Wing Tsit. Chinese Philosophy, Princeton University Press, Princeton, 1963

Chinweizu. The West and the Rest of Us, Rando Press, New York,   1973

Ciarke, John Henrik. AfRaKan World Revolution, Africa World Press, New Jersey, 1991

Clan, Mossi Warrior. Killmonger's Corner: The Conscious Community Pan African Journal Vol. 2, by Blak Pantha (Author), Khufu Mentuhotep (Author), Michael Hope (Author), Ini-Herit N/A (Author), Kofi Piesie (Author), Asar Hotep (Author), Brother Seneb (Author), Jaycee Hughes (Author), Aliyma Njie (Author), Sheree Swann

Davis, Angela. Women, Race, And Class, Vintage Books   New York, 1983

Diop, Cheikh Anta. Civilization or Barbarism, Presence Africaine, Paris, 1991

Diop, Cheikh Anta. The Cultural Unity of Black Africa, Third World Press, 1978

Douglass, Frederick. Narrative of the Life of Frederick Douglass-An American Slave, New American Library, New York, 1968

Dubois, W.E.B., The Souls of Black Polk, revised edition, Nal Penguin Inc., New York, 1969

Dubois, W.E.B., The Autobiography of W.E.B. Dubois, International Publishers, U.S.A., 1968

Fanon, Frantz. Wretched of the Earth, Presence Africaine, Paris, 1963

Frazier, E. Franklin. The Black Church in America, by Schocken Books Inc., New York, 1974

Freire, Paulo, Pedagogy of the Oppressed, The
Continuum Publishing Corporation, New York,
1985

Gbadegesin, Segun. African Philpsophy, Peter
lang' New York, 1991

George, Nelson. The death of Rhythm and
Blues, Penguin Group, New York,1988   ,

Green, David. translation of Ammi, Ben
God,the Black Man and Truth, Communication
Press Chicago, 1982

Habermas, Jurgen. On the Logic of Social
Sciences, trans by Shierry Nicholson and Jerry
Stark, M.I.T Press Cambridge, 1989

Habermas, Jurgen. Knowledge and Human
Interests, Beacon Press NewYork, 1989

Hadjor, Kofi Buenor. Tranforming Africa: Discourse with Africa's Leaders, Africa World Press, New Jersey, 1987

Hampshire, Stuart. The Age of Reason, Meridian, New York, 1956

Harding, Vincent. There is a River, Vintage Books, New York, 1983

Harris, Leonard. Philosophy Born of Struggle, Kendall/Hunt Pub., Iowa, 1983

Heilbroner, Robert L., Marxism, For and Against, W. W. Norton, New York, 1980

Higgins, Kathleen Marie. Nietzche's Zarathustra, Temple University Press, Philadelphia, 1987

Holloway, Joseph E., Africanisms in American Culture, Indiana University Press, Bloomington, 1991

Jackson, John G., Man, God and Civilization, Citadel Press, New Jersey, 1972

James, George G.M., Stolen Legacy, United Brothers Communications Systems, Virginia, 1989

Jones, Leroi. Blues People, Morrow Quill, New York, 1963

Jowet, B, trans. The Dialogues of Plato, volume II, Random House, New York, 1937

Kant, Immanuel., The Critique of Pure Reason,Trans. by Norman Kemp Smith, St. Martin's Press, New York 1986

Obenga, Theophile, African Philosophy, Brawtley Press, U.S.A 2015

Patterson, D.E Narmer's Palette, by Palamon & Arcite

Poetry, A division of Palamon & Arcite.

Piesie, Kofie., Beautiful Lessons About
Kimoyo, Same Tree Different Branch
Publishing, U.S.A 2021

Reid, Garfield. Misconceptions &
Misinformation by the Black Hebrew Israelites
Vol. 1, Reid, 2021

Sartre, Jean Paul. Essays in Exi1tentialism,
Carol Pub., New York, 1965.

Serequeberhan, Tsenay. "Karl Marx and
African Emanicipatory Thought: A Critique of
Marx's Eurocentric Metaphysics, Praxis
International, 10:1/2, April and July, 1990

Taylor Charles. Hegel, Cambrigde University
Press, New York, 1995

Tucker, Robert. The Marx/Engels Reader,
second edition, W.W. Norton & Company, 1978

Van Sertima, Ivan. Blacks in Science, Transaction Book New Brunswick, 1992

Van Sertima, Ivan. AfRaKan Presence in Early America Journal of AfRaKan Civilizations Ltd., 1987 '

Van Sertima, Ivan. Great AfRaKan Thinkers, Transaction Books, New Brunswick, 1987

Walker, Alice. You Can't Keep A Good Arabinrin Down, Harcourt Brace Jovanovich Pub., New York, 1981

Welsing, Frances Cress. The Isis Papers, Third World Press, Chicago, 1991

West, Ankh. The Chronology of Human Evolution: Real Black Atheism Explained Voices of Fire Press, St. Louis, Missouri, 2016

West, Cornel. Prophetic Fragments, William Eardmanns

Pub., Michigan,   1988

Wikipedia. https://en.wikipedia.org/wiki/ Caucasus_Mountains

Williams,   Chancellor. The Destruction of Black Civilization, revised edition, Chicago, Third World Press, 1987

Wilmore, Gayraud S., Black Religion and Black Radicalism, second edition, Orbis Books, New York, 1973

Wright,. Richard. African Philosophy, third edition, University Press of America, Maryland, 1984

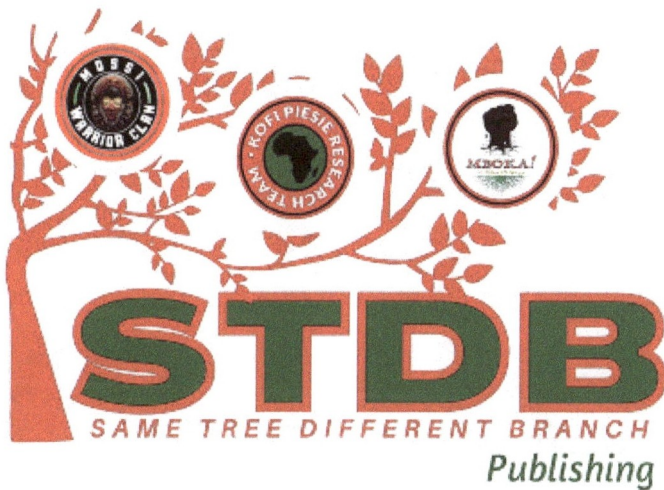